CONTENTS

D0771595

Electric Bass

One evening in the middle of 1951 a solitary light burns in the otherwise darkened Fender workshops on Pomona Avenue. Leo Fender is working the night away, oblivious to family dining and other everyday activities across the rest of Fullerton, near Los Angeles.

Leo is fiddling yet again with the string-length of his new baby. On the bench before him sits a prototype guitar which, in a few short months, will go on sale as the Fender Precision Bass. Today, we know that it was to become his most revolutionary product. But Leo is unaware of this as he carefully screws the latest new neck to the scarred prototype body.

The emerging sound of rock'n'roll would have been impossible had Leo not toiled on that night and many other occasions. Bearing in mind non-musician Leo's own taste in music – singing cowboys The Sons Of The Pioneers were his favourites – then maybe he would have consigned the prototype to his trashcan, given what it led to.

Fortunately for us he persevered. Fender's idea for a bass guitar was almost unprecedented – not to say downright shocking. Of course, bass is as old as music itself. It began long ago, probably when people first started to sing together and noticed that some of them had lower voices, which made a good foundation to underpin and strengthen their music. Maybe they got the same kick singing bass parts as we do now when we play bass guitar.

There's something unique about providing the bass, about adding a bassline to the music. It's a shivers-up-the-spine moment when you get it right. It's subversive, too. A bassline can completely shift the mood and intention of a

Linkin Park's Dave 'Phoenix' Farrell, with Music Man StingRay

piece, altering the framework and taking the music somewhere else. It's what Paul McCartney tells us is "the power the bass player has within the band. Not vengeful power, just that you can actually control it".[1]

In this book, we'll mainly be talking about the bass in popular music. Not that bass doesn't turn up in all kinds of music, but it's in pop, rock, jazz, blues, country and the rest that the real revolution has taken place. All the modern variants and fusions and sub-genres of these styles would not sound the way they do if it were not for the electric bass guitar. This book is a celebration of that wonderful instrument.

And yes, we'll be talking almost exclusively about the electric bass guitar. Before we start, however, we should mention its predecessor, the double bass (or upright bass), which has a long and distinguished history. Most experts date it back to Europe in the early 1500s. Since then, musicians and makers have established it as the largest and lowest-tuned member of the violin family (which means it was originally designed to be played with a bow). Its most important musical settings today are in jazz and classical music.

As the bowed and plucked anchor at the bottom of the string section in the modern symphony orchestra, the double bass began to appear from the early 18th century, as well as in jazz and ragtime groups and string bands. In America in the 1920s it took over from the tuba (or improvised instruments such as the washtub bass) as the principal bass instrument and, mainly as a plucked instrument, it quickly spread to other popular-music bands.

In the beginning

And so we come to our beloved electric bass guitar. Now then, where did it begin, and how? Who played it when it first appeared? In short, what we really need to find out is how we got to where we are today.

To start to understand all this, we first ought to go back to the late 1940s. Picture the American guitarist back then. Maybe he's playing an acoustic guitar, but more likely he's got an amplified guitar, especially if he plays blues or jazz or western swing. In a large band, he'll need one just to compete with the volume of the rest of the players, although the swing and jazz big-band era is fading, and increasingly the work he gets is in smaller groups.

Our guitarist finds that one way of getting more work is to be able to play an additional instrument, but he's used to the size and the comfort of his fretted guitar. When he tries a double bass he struggles to keep good pitch on that big, fretless instrument, nicknamed the doghouse because of its awkward size.

Now picture the double bass player in America at the same time. All around him the rhythm section is getting louder: the drum kit is growing in size to project the music's pulse, and guitarists have become accustomed to using the amplified electric guitars that first appeared in the previous decade. Our bass player enjoys no such technology. He's saddled with the unwieldy acoustic double bass and is still having trouble being heard over the musical noise generated by the rest of his band.

When, against this background, the Fender Electric Instrument Co of Fullerton, near Los Angeles, California, introduced a solidbody electric bass guitar toward the end of 1951, nobody really knew what to make of the strange hybrid. It looked like a long-necked version of Fender's Telecaster solidbody electric guitar, which the company had just launched. But the new Fender Precision Bass had four strings on a long neck and was tuned like a double bass in fourths to E-A-D-G, an octave below the lower four strings of a guitar. Those who saw this new instrument gazed at a peculiar, unfamiliar thing.

Leo Fender's idea for a bass guitar was certainly radical, but the idea of an amplified bass was somewhat longer in the tooth.

Thirty years earlier, in the 1920s, Lloyd Loar, an engineer at the Gibson Mandolin-Guitar Co in Kalamazoo, Michigan, experimented with a slimmed-down electric double bass.

In the 1930s, Rickenbacker in California marketed a stick-shaped electric upright bass ("held upright or in playing position by our new folding adjustable stand"[2]), as did Regal of Chicago ("fine for all fretted groups as well as orchestras"[3]) and Vega of Boston ("bass players have been looking for an Electric Bass to enhance their own position and to give the orchestra greater bass foundation"[4]). None of these efforts was commercially successful and none of them was helped by the poor quality of amplification available at the time. Makers seemed to know that bass players wanted a louder instrument but had trouble finding a suitable way of helping them.

In the late 1940s, New York bassist Everett Hull approached the problem from a more practical angle. He reasoned that you could take the existing upright bass and amplify that. So he began to produce an amplification system for acoustic double basses consisting of a microphone that fitted inside the bass's pointed peg, the spike that supports it at the base of the body. This 'amplified peg' gave the company its name, and Ampeg's adaptation of existing double basses to amplified sound was a moderate success.

Four-string guitars had hit the North American market well in advance of Fender's 1951 Precision, although they were quite different in style and purpose. In the 1920s, companies such as Gibson (again) and Martin of

Nazareth, Pennsylvania, came up with the acoustic tenor guitar. Rickenbacker and Vega later made electric versions. These tenor guitars certainly weren't bass guitars. They sported four strings tuned C-D-G-A on a narrow neck, an arrangement intended to encourage banjo players to move from the old-guard banjo to the newly popular guitar.

Martin slightly confused our history lesson soon after that by briefly calling their Dreadnought six-string flat-top acoustics of the 1930s 'bass guitars' – but only because these new large-body instruments had a more bassy tone than usual, designed to suit vocal accompaniment.

Deep, profound pulsations

It turns out that the idea of a fretted bass wasn't new either. Ancient multi-string fretted bass instruments such as the bass lute and theorbo date back to the 1600s, but at the beginning of the 20th century, Gibson made a small number of the four-string fretted Mando Bass, continuing for 20 years or so from the early 1910s.

A late-1920s Gibson catalogue shows a dinner-suited musician playing the acoustic Mando Bass with a pick and holding the instrument guitar-style across his body thanks to the support of a metal rod, which protrudes from the lower side of the instrument and rests on the floor. The Mando Bass had a two-foot wide pear-shape body, a round soundhole, four strings tuned E-A-D-G, a 42-inch scale-length (the average for a double bass), and 17 frets.

"Listen to modern music as played for dance, concert, recording, or radio and you will find that the bass is one of the most important instruments, adding to the ensemble the deep, profound pulsations that are the heart and soul of true rhythm," suggested Gibson's catalogue in a timeless phrase.[5]

Gibson described the fretted Mando Bass as "unusually easy to play", but what they didn't tell the budding bassist of the 1920s was that this $150 instrument did little to project its sound through the band and into the audience. Consequently it was not a great success during its surprisingly long life – Leo Fender knew a local band who used a Mando Bass in the 1940s.

There is even evidence of an electric bass guitar pre-dating Fender's Precision. Paul Tutmarc, a Hawaiian guitar player and teacher based in Seattle, Washington, set up a company called Audiovox in the 1930s to manufacture electric instruments, including an electric bass guitar. The Model 736 Bass Fiddle is shown in Audiovox's leaflet dating from around 1936. It had a roughly guitar-shape walnut body, a single pickup and control knob on a pearloid pickguard, a neck with 16 frets, and a cord emerging from a jack on the upper side of the body. This was an astonishingly early electric bass guitar design, and Tutmarc must be noted at least as a man with remarkable foresight if little commercial luck.

Tutmarc's son, Bud, later marketed a very similar electric bass guitar, called the Serenader, through the L.D. Heater music distribution company of Portland, Oregon. Heater's undated flyer describes the $139.50 Serenader electric bass guitar as "designed to eliminate the bulkiness of a regular size bass viol" ('bass viol' was another term for double bass). Bud claimed that the Serenader bass guitar was launched in 1948.

None of this detracts from the significance and importance of Fender's introduction of the solidbody electric Precision Bass guitar in 1951. The Audiovox and Serenader basses, even if they really were first, made no impact on the market or on music. In contrast, by the late 1950s and into the early 1960s, Fender's electric bass guitars would become the industry standard, providing a solid foundation to the new sound of pop music.

The Precision arrives, precisely

Leo Fender was born in 1909 in the Fullerton–Anaheim area of Southern California. His parents were orange growers, and Leo was born in the barn they had built (a house followed the next year). Despite working as a young man as an accountant, Leo grew to love electronics and ham radio, and he would build amplifiers and public address systems for outdoor sports events and similar gatherings in the Orange County area.

In the late 1930s, Leo opened a radio store, Fender Radio Service, in Fullerton. He sold electrical gear, records, musical instruments, PA systems, and sheet music, as well as offering a repair service. He found this put him in touch with many local musicians. One in particular, violinist and lap-steel guitarist 'Doc' Kauffman, teamed up with Leo in a shortlived company and they began producing K&F (Kauffman and Fender) electric lap-steel guitars and amplifiers in 1945.

By February of the following year, Kauffman had left, unsettled by Leo's workaholic methods and the precarious finances of the project. Leo set up his own operation later in 1946, at first calling it Fender Manufacturing and renaming it the Fender Electric Instrument Co in December 1947.

He continued to make and sell the line of lap-steels and amps as he had with K&F and soon moved production work into two steel buildings on nearby South Pomona Avenue. It was here that Leo survived near-crippling cashflow problems to come up with his Esquire six-string solidbody electric guitar and the Fender Precision Bass. The company added a good new bass amplifier to partner the instrument, the Bassman model.

Fender's Precision was launched during the closing months of 1951, starting in October (although it wasn't officially shown to the musical instruments trade until the July 1952 NAMM show, at the Hotel New Yorker in New York City). The new bass shared much of the style of its construction with Fender's new solidbody electric guitar, which during 1951 had been renamed the Telecaster.

The Precision had a 20-fret maple neck bolted to a slab ash body, which was painted in a pale yellow colour. The narrow headstock had four big-key Kluson tuners. The body had a black plastic pickguard and finger-rest plus a four-pole single-coil pickup. There was a chromed metal plate with a volume and tone control, plus a chromed cover each for the pickup and (with built-in rubber mute underneath) the bridge. The bridge had two saddles, each carrying two strings. The strings passed over the bridge and through the body, anchored at the rear. The body had two cutaways, the first Fender guitar with such a design.

The new bass had an austere simplicity and was geared to easy construction, which was typical of the early products from Fender. Leo would always opt for function over looks. "I had so many years of experience with work on radios and electronic gear," he said, "and my main interest was in the utility aspects of an item – that was the main thing. Appearance came next. That gets turned around sometimes."6

Leo also knew the importance of simplicity in design to ease repair and service problems. His years in the radio store had taught him a lot. "The design of everything we did was intended to be easy to build and easy to repair," he said later. "When I was in the repair business, dealing with other men's problems, I could see the shortcomings in a design, completely disregarding the need for service. If a thing is easy to service, it is easy to build."7

All the principal design elements were shown in Leo Fender's patent for "the ornamental design" of the Precision Bass. He applied for it in November 1952 and it was issued on March 24th 1953. The electric bass guitar had arrived ... and nobody took much notice.

Today, many years after Leo Fender's death, it's impossible to know exactly his motivation for introducing the Precision, but we can make some informed guesses. Did he, for example, expect to sell the instrument to double bass players or to guitarists? Probably both, of course. "Anyone with the necessary $199.50" might well have been Leo's reply. In today's money, that retail price would be equivalent to about $1,550.

Most people who were there at the time say that Leo first determined a need for such an instrument mainly by talking to the musicians who came and went at the Fullerton workshops and who played in and around town (including Jack Kelleher, a local big-band and western swing bassist). The guitarists among them realised that playing more than one instrument increased their employment opportunities – and any who'd tried the big double bass generally found it hard to play.

As usual in the early years, Leo relied heavily on these local players. They would try out prototypes and testbed instruments that Fender supplied, giving their opinions on this pickup arrangement or that control scheme. Leo remembered: "About 25 percent of every day was spent with visiting musicians, trying to figure out what would suit their needs best."[8] One guinea pig said how he'd often turn around on stage at a local gig to see Leo "oblivious of musicians, audience, club management, and disruption generally," busily changing amp controls or suggesting instrument settings – and usually in mid-song.[9]

Maybe the name of the new Fender bass was a come-on to guitarists and others who considered the unfretted neck of the double bass too imprecise? Don Randall was general manager of Radio & Television Equipment Co, Fender's distributor in the early 1950s, and soon to become a key person in the growing Fender operation. He recalls that the Precision name was more a typical concoction of Leo Fender's technically-oriented mind.

Randall named all the Fender products except the Precision, and he remembers how that came about. "Leo and I had a discussion about the new bass, and he's telling me how precision it was, how you could fret it right down to a hundredth of an inch. Now who puts their finger a hundredth of an inch this way or that on a bass string? But he was so possessed with the fact that this was the first time that the fret layout on a bass was so precise. He said to me, 'You know, it's so precise we ought to call it the precision bass.' Well, why not? So it became the Fender Precision Bass."[10]

Many years after the event, Leo said: "When you're a guitar player and you play [double bass] you have to listen to the pitch: ordinarily your ears are at the end of the bass, because it stands upright. You have difficulties hearing the pitch because the drums and the other parts of the orchestra are so loud. … So we made the Fender bass, and the guitar player didn't have to worry about the pitch when he played with other instruments."[11]

Setting the scale

Some of Fender's early promotional material seems designed to remind double bass players that they too could benefit from the new instrument. For example, one of the first U.S. music-trade press features on the Precision Bass, in April 1952, was headed 'Fender Bass and Amplifier Replace Old Style in 1/6 Size'. The report quoted Fender's press release: "The Precision four-string bass is a considerable departure from the old style standard bass in that it is only one-sixth the standard size and is played in the same position as a guitar, supported from the neck. … The neck is slender and fretted, which enables considerable ease and comfort for the player." The reference to one-sixth standard size sounds like a confusion, but the point about this being a new, more portable bass is well made.

Speaking more recently, Randall remembers that the new Precision Bass wasn't only aimed at guitarists. "The guitar players picked it up, of course, and many of them played bass and guitar, but most of the guys in the travelling bands were playing the big bass. They had to have a moving van to take everything where they were going! The Fender was a godsend to them. It wasn't so cumbersome as the big acoustic bass."

Fender's press info continued: "A finger style of playing is used rather than the old style of slapping and jerking the strings, which was necessary with the older style instrument to obtain sufficient volume. This new instrument when used with the Bassman amplifier produces considerably more volume than a conventional [double] bass, and with a great deal less effort on the part of the player. Bass players will find that they are less tired after a night of playing the Fender Precision Bass than with the older type."[12]

The tuning of the Fender bass, E-A-D-G, was the same as the double bass and an octave below the lower four strings of the guitar. These familiarities were designed to attract both sets of players.

A question we can't now ask Leo is why he chose the scale-length of 34 inches for his Precision. The scale length of a guitar is the distance from nut to bridge saddle and therefore determines the sounding length of the string and its relative tension, tone, and playability.

The 34-inch scale-length of Fender's new electric bass guitar was around nine inches longer than that of most conventional six-string guitars, a requirement derived from the much deeper pitch of the instrument, and about eight inches shorter than the average scale-length of a double bass.

George Fullerton worked for Leo with only a few breaks from early 1948 through to Fender's death in 1991. Fullerton said that during the original experiments to determine the scale length of the Precision they tried shorter scales, such as 30 and 32 inches. "But they didn't seem to get the resonance we needed. We may even have tried something like a 36-inch scale, but when we got to that length the distance between the frets was too wide to be practical for a player."[13]

Randall agrees that trial and error were the major factors in determining the scale-length. "It didn't have any basis in science, that's for sure!" he laughs. "I think it just probably evolved from trying to see what was the most convenient scale to play." Randall also points to another early problem: a lack of strings for the new instrument. "We had to go through some rigmaroles to get them because, simply, they weren't being made. It was either Mapes or Squier who made the first proper ones for us."[14]

The Precision's body design was new for Fender, with an extra cutaway on the upper body compared to the company's existing Telecaster shape, and the new style would inspire the body outline of Fender's later Stratocaster guitar. Fullerton recalls a practical reason for the cutaway, even if most players knew it meant easier access to higher frets.

"For the Precision Bass we pretty much followed the Telecaster shape," says Fullerton. "The reason for the extra cutaway was the strap – because on the upper side you don't need a cutaway anyhow. This longer neck on the bass and the heavier keys made it overbalanced, and so by extending the top horn you put the suspension for the location of the strap holder more in the centre, to offset the balance.

"All these things were designed into it for a particular reason: we wouldn't just say oh, I'm gonna put a horn on it. But in those days nothing was available, for instance there were no bass keys available. We used to take great big keys that fit on those hollow basses and cut them down to make them fit."[15]

Chubby sees the electric future

In those years at the start of the 1950s, few other guitar companies took seriously Fender's new direction with the electric bass. Forrest White, who worked as Fender's production chief from 1954, remembers a salesman telling him about the reaction to the Precision Bass at an early trade show. "Anyone who had wondered whether Leo was crazy or not, well – now they knew he was crazy. Who in the world is gonna play an electric bass?"[16]

One exception was the Kay company of Chicago, best known for cheap and cheerful guitars and equally budget-conscious double basses. With this particular combination of market interests, Kay became the first to join Fender, quickly adding a bass guitar model to their line. Kay launched their K-162 'electronic' bass guitar in 1952 at the same summer NAMM convention in New York City where Fender first showed the Precision to the trade.

Big-band leader Woody Herman's bass player Chubby Jackson had been associated with Kay since 1945, when the company issued a 'signature' double bass, the S-51 Chubby Jackson five-string model, which he would often use amplified. He is pictured in Kay publicity of the time wearing a bemused grin as he tries Kay's $150 short-scale electric bass guitar.

A reporter, clearly baffled by the brand new development, was allowed to sit in on Jackson's demonstration of the Kay bass at the '52 trade show. "Kay sprang its surprise instrument when [a sales manager] handed Chubby an instrument resembling a guitar. This unusual instrument was a miniature [double bass] which, when plugged in to the [amplifier], had the same range and tone of its big brother. The only real difference, as Chubby said, was that he could sit down to play the miniature.

"Chubby extolled the new instrument, although he did say that he would have to practice on it before considering himself truly capable of playing it. The finger action of both hands is changed in switching from a bass to a guitar, he explained. He told his audience, with a wry smile, that he could see his own instrument and career going to pot now that all guitar players could easily become bass players also."[17] Jackson could not have known just how prophetic his casual remarks would turn out to be.

Bass player Donald 'Duck' Dunn started out in the 1950s with one of those early Kay bass guitars. He would go on to fame in the 1960s with a Fender communicating his beautifully solid support to music by Booker T & The MGs, Otis Redding, Sam & Dave, and others.

A few more years into the 1950s and Kay offered a new bass, the K-160, this time with a strange D-G-B-E tuning, "the same as the first four strings of a Spanish guitar except one octave lower". This concoction did not last.

But all this underlines the fact that the pioneering makers of the early 1950s were still not at all sure what an electric bass was or exactly what players should use it for. Players too were suspicious of this weird new thing. Some double bass players figured that anything with frets was somehow 'cheating' and not worthy of their consideration, although some could already see the big changes that the electric bass would make. Some guitarists began to think that as the bass guitar had fewer strings, somehow it must be an instrument for second-rate musicians. This was the start of a stigma that was to last for some time.

Hampton's surging undertow

One of the earliest musicians to use the electric bass guitar in a popular setting was Roy Johnson of the Lionel Hampton Band. This news was revealed in the first important publicity for the Fender Precision Bass, less than nine months after it had appeared. In July 1952, the U.S. jazz magazine *Down Beat* featured a photograph of jazz vibraphonist and big-band leader Lionel Hampton posing with a Fender Precision Bass.

Hampton's big-band of the time combined swing and R&B in a sort of early jazz–rock'n'roll fusion. Hampton emphasised crowd-pleasing solos, rhythmic grooves, and a punchy brass section. He was unusually open to new ideas and new ways of performing music – exactly the kind of broadminded setting where the innovative electric bass guitar might flourish.

In that issue of *Down Beat*, below the picture of Hamp and the bass, was a report by the noted jazz journalist Leonard Feather, headed "Hamp-lified Fiddle May Lighten Bassists' Burdens". (Double basses were also referred to as 'bass fiddles'.) Feather suggested that a bass revolution was underway. Players would no longer have to lug around a heavy, cumbersome instrument.

"It first became apparent some months ago when Lionel Hampton's band played a gig in [New York City]," wrote Feather. "Suddenly we observed that there was something wrong with the band. It didn't have a bass player. And yet – we heard a bass.

"On second glance we noticed something even odder. There were two guitars – but we only heard one. And then the picture became clearer.

"Sitting next to the guitarist," Feather continued, "was someone who held what looked like a guitar at first glance, but on closer inspection revealed a long, fretted neck and a peculiarly shaped body, with electric controls and a wire running to a speaker. 'Sure man,' said Hamp excitedly when we asked him later, 'that's our electric bass. We've had it for months!' He introduced us to Roy Johnson, the Kansas City bassist who for all these months had been trudging around the country, unheralded, playing this sensational instrumental innovation. But Johnson has himself a whale of a plaything – a whale built like a sprat, to boot."[18]

The reporter then described the sound of the weird new bass in a timeless sentence. Feather was an able witness to the first signs of a sound that would change music. "[I was] duly impressed by the deep, booming quality," he wrote, "the ability to make astonishing glissandi, and the way the bass, its volume turned up a little above normal, cut through the whole bottom of the band with a surging undertow."

Johnson left Hampton's band, but the idea of the electric Precision Bass stayed. Hamp's next bassman was William 'Monk' Montgomery, brother of guitarist Wes. Fender's Don Randall remembers him very well. "Monk was the guy who really got us off the ground with our electric bass," he says. Fender would spotlight a stylish drawing of Monk and his Precision in a later catalogue.

Randall: "The Hampton band made a European tour and we got some glowing reports back from Monk. He would write me and say boy, it's going down well. In fact he was getting all the notoriety that Hampton should have got, because everybody was overwhelmed by this guy playing an electric bass. We got newspaper clippings from all over western Europe."[19]

That tour started in September 1953 in Norway. Britain's *Melody Maker* headlined its report "Hampton Knocks 'em Out At Oslo Debut" and underneath was a prominent picture of Monk playing his Fender Precision Bass at the concert alongside the guitarist. The caption underneath the photograph read: "Not Two Guitars: The duettists are William Mackel on guitar with William Montgomery – on electric bass."[20]

Monk adds a depth to the rhythm

Still, nobody knew quite what to make of this weird new instrument. As Hampton's European tour continued, more reports appeared. Ralph Berton wrote about the October 1953 Paris date and seemed in awe when it came to Monk Montgomery. "He produced some really inspiring sounds on an electrically amplified bass," said Berton, "which resembled a large guitar."[21]

A month later, in the wake of all the interest generated by Montgomery's bass guitar, *Melody Maker* asked a panel of evidently conservative British double bass players what they thought of the new-fangled device. The reactions were unanimous. "Frankly, I don't see the point," said one. Another: "It looks nothing like a bass and can only sound like an electric guitar." One said: "It can only be a weak note amplified." And another: "It can never produce a perfect sound; all you get is an amplified plink-plonk." And so on, confirming the horrified reaction.[22]

But Montgomery got the last word. Tracked down at London Airport on a stopover on his way home to America with the Hampton band, Montgomery was shown these criticisms by a brave journalist. Montgomery shrugged them off. "It's the greatest thing that happened," he told Mike Nevard. "I joined Hamp with an ordinary bass, but he liked the electric kind. His last bass man had one; he said I ought to get one. I didn't like the idea at all, but I got one. Boy was I glad! I had to start learning all over again, but there's nothing like it. The whole thing about it is that you get a better tone. And since our piano player left, I've found even more advantages. For instance, the electric model seems to fill in a lot for the missing piano: it gives a kind of depth to the rhythm that's missing when the piano's not there. I play a Fender. It's not a special job: a California firm turns it out."[23]

Why was Hampton so keen to have the avant-garde electric bass in his band? Montgomery said it was because Hampton liked the sound and volume of the instrument. "Because he could hear the bass, really hear the bass. When there's an upright bass in the band, you don't really hear it as much as you feel it. ... The instrument blends into the music, it isn't dominant. Hamp used to come back to my amp and turn it up. You know how Hamp would sort of prance or parade in front of the band? That happy sound, and he'd be sweating and the music getting to him ... and he'd clap his way over to the amp and turn it up because he wanted more bass, I guess. He liked that sound."[24] It seems as if Hampton was an early rock'n'roller in jazz disguise. No wonder he was one of the first musicians to turn on to the electric bass.

Montgomery continued, with a handful of exceptions, to play his Fender bass in jazz settings, a rarity until jazz-rock came along at the end of the 1960s. In a 1957 interview, he explained the advantages of bass guitar over upright. "I don't get tired playing it. It's so much less work; it's more accurate and you can have more speed. I can't play a tempo that's too fast for it. And I can't run a clear scale on a big bass."[25]

Gibson takes the plunge

Gradually, more guitar makers cottoned on and began to produce bass models. Gibson put out their Electric Bass toward the end of 1953 (the first one left the factory in early September). It had a solid mahogany violin-shape body, evidently designed to appeal to double bass players, who would certainly recognise the look. This short-scale bass had an optional 'spike' that fitted to the bottom of the body and allowed the bassist to play the instrument upright ... like a double bass. It was rarely used – but nonetheless remained a feature well into the 1960s, and not only on the Gibson. Gretsch, among others, offered a body-spike too. It's another indication of the continuing confusion over who would be playing the new bass guitar.

Ted McCarty, president of Gibson at the time, said they made the Electric Bass because their salesmen were asked for such an instrument, presumably as a result of the Fender and Kay electric bass guitars already on the market. Gibson's 'violin' design was copied a few years later, albeit with a hollow body, by the German company Hofner. This probably would have failed to make the history books had it not been adopted in 1961 by a young British musician named Paul McCartney – of whom more later.

■ A rare early newspaper cutting (left) shows **Leo Fender** at his firm's workshops in California in November 1952. Leo is pictured proudly holding the new Fender Precision Bass. "Even a five-year-old could cart around this compact, 50-pound bass fiddle," ran the paper's caption. Fender's sales chief Don Randall (above, centre) shows off the new bass at a 1952 instrument trade show in New York City.

■ At first, Fender's ads were plain and to the point, like the one for the new Precision (above) that appeared early in 1952. The patent (right) for the general design of the Precision Bass was issued in 1953 to Clarence Leo Fender, his full name.

Fender
PRECISION BASS

■ **Fender Precision Bass 1951** Leo Fender's small company in Fullerton, Los Angeles, started the entire bass guitar business with this revolutionary item. No longer was the bassist rooted to one spot on stage with a bulky acoustic 'doghouse' double bass.

The Precison name came from the fretted fingerboard that gave players precise pitching. This rare example is one of the earliest to have survived from the first weeks of production. The body is dated October 30th and the neck November 20th 1951.

Gibson added a few more short-scale bass guitars to their catalogue later in the 1950s, including in 1958 the EB-2, which was a bass version of the company's new ES-335 guitar. It shared the 335's new body design, a development of Gibson's slim-body 'thinline' style, but now with a radical double-cutaway design as well as a novel solid block within the otherwise hollow body to create a new 'semi-solid' structure.

Gibson's idea with the EB-2 (and the 335) was effectively to combine a hollowbody guitar with a solidbody, not only in terms of construction but also in sonic effect. The EB-2's solid maple block inside what Gibson described as a "wonder-thin" body offered hollowbody and solidbody tones in one instrument.

At the same time, Gibson renamed the violin-shape Electric Bass the EB-1, but dropped it the following year, replacing it with the solidbody EB-0 (effectively a bass version of Gibson's double-cutaway Les Paul Junior guitar).

Gibson seemed to view their bass models as mere four-string versions of what they considered the far more important guitar models, and the company indulged guitarists who wanted to play bass by only offering bass guitars with short 30-inch scale-lengths.

Six-string bass – take one

New Yorker Nathan Daniel produced his first Danelectro guitars in 1954, at first mainly building instruments under the Silvertone brand for the Sears Roebuck mail-order company. Daniel's instruments were boldly styled and, while cheap and using basic materials such as masonite (hardboard), worked surprisingly well.

Around 1956, Danelectro produced the first six-string electric bass guitar, the UB-1 (single-pickup) or UB-2 (double-pickup), effectively a guitar tuned an octave lower than usual. Like other early bass guitars from Kay and Gibson, the Dan'o had a short scale (29 inches). At the time, Fender was still the only maker offering a bass with a 'full' 34-inch scale. A longer scale-length generally means that string tension is tighter, in turn giving a better focus to each note, improved overall sustain, and a more tangible bass-end to the sound.

The single-cutaway Danelectro six-string also featured a two-octave, 24-fret fingerboard that was unusual for the time. Guitarists were the target for this instrument, evident from Danelectro's catalogue that introduced the UB-2 as "a six-string guitar with extra-long neck and fingerboard, and extra-long strings".[26]

Nathan Daniel said: "People started making bass guitars, and it was no big deal for us to switch from guitars to basses: we simply made the neck a bit longer. We started with a six-string bass because it's hardly any more trouble than a four-string and it gave the player something more for the same money. It took time for that to catch on, but if the player was capable, he had more stuff to play with."[27]

Danelectro went on to add a very distinctive bass to their catalogue in 1959, the 24-fret Long Horn model, available in four-string and six-string versions, which joined the slightly earlier and more conservative Short Horn bass with just 15 frets. (Reissues of all the popular Dano's would start to appear in 1998.)

For a great period example of Danelectro six-string bass on record, listen to Duane Eddy's 'Because They're Young' (recorded January 1960 with a Long Horn) or hop forward to Glen Campbell's 'Wichita Lineman' (1968). Session bassist Carol Kaye says she loaned Campbell her six-string Danelectro bass for the gorgeous solo. Kaye played on Ritchie Valens's raucous 1958 hit 'La Bamba', and it sounds suspiciously as if that's a Dan'o six-string bass in there attempting to hold the chaos together.

Other companies added six-string basses to their line: Gibson in 1959 with the $340 hollowbody EB-6 and Fender in 1961 with the $329.50 solid Bass VI. Fender's press release for the new VI insisted that "both guitarists and bassists should find it easy to play".[28]

But the VI and others like it were still essentially 'baritone' guitars: in others words regular six-string guitars down an octave, aimed principally at guitar players (and quite different from our modern idea of a six-string bass). None was especially successful, although the Danelectro was popular in a specialist studio role, and British bassist Jack Bruce would briefly use a Fender Bass VI in his early Cream days in the 1960s before moving on to a four-string Gibson EB-3. Glen Campbell performed 'Wichita Lineman' on television around the time of its release playing a Fender VI.

Some years later, John Entwistle tried to use a Danelectro for his bass solo on The Who's 1965 single 'My Generation'. "So as to get the right effect, I had to buy a Danelectro bass, because it has thin little strings that produce a very twangy sound," said Entwistle.[29] But the strings broke easily and, as no replacements were available in London, he simply went and bought two more Dan'o basses after breaking strings during the recording of early takes.

Eventually he gave up and made the released version with a Fender Jazz Bass – strung, surprisingly given the sound, with LaBella flatwound strings. The result, released in late 1965, was the first hit single A-side to feature an electric bass solo (or to be more precise, a series of bass breaks).

Entwistle went on in the 1960s to pioneer the new 'roundwound' strings from British company Rotosound. Bass guitarists could now choose between

■ **Gibson Electric Bass 1953** (above) Gibson's first bass guitar was firmly traditional, like a scaled-down double bass. Meanwhile, Fender attracted players like **Monk Montgomery** (right).

Monk Montgomery

REVELATION IN RHYTHM

Gibson electric bass

Dave Reiser, popular bass guitarist of the Reiser Brothers Trio.

Leading combos, western and country groups are featuring a "new sound" ... the Gibson electric bass. Gibson's renowned electronic department is proud of this instrumental innovation, heralded for its deep, sustaining tones, lightning fast action and ease of handling. Teamed with the new Gibson GA-90 Hi-Fi Amplifier, with six speakers, here's really a "revelation in rhythm".

GIBSON, INC., Kalamazoo, Michigan

12   METRONOME

■ Gibson EB-2 1960
Later in the 1950s, Gibson launched this model at the same time as its ES-335 guitar. Both were made in the company's new 'semi-solid' style. A wooden block runs through the centre of the otherwise hollow body, giving the tonality of both solid and hollow guitars in one bass. Fender at this time did not offer a hollowbody bass. (The cherry finish on this EB-2 is unusual: most were seen in natural wood or shaded sunburst finish.)

■ Gibson's Electric Bass (1954 ad, above) was later renamed the EB-1. The 'violin bass' recalled the cumbersome acoustic double bass that the electric variety was supposed to replace. Gibson even provided a telescopic spike so that the EB-1 could still be played upright, and rear-facing 'banjo' tuners (seen in the close-up, centre) helped to dispel any notion that Gibson were following the electric bass template established by Fender earlier in the 1950s.

23

the traditional tones of the established flatwound strings or the bright, bell-like sound of the new roundwounds.

Rickenbacker joins the club

The Rickenbacker company of California had been an early yet frustrated pioneer with electric upright basses. In 1953, founder Adolph Rickenbacker sold his company to Francis Hall, whose Radio & Television Equipment Co distributed Fender's early products. Hall's business relationship with Fender ended soon after he bought Rickenbacker. He set about modernising and revamping the Rickenbacker product line, principally through the efforts of German-born guitar maker Roger Rossmeisl, who joined the West Coast company early in 1954.

Rickenbacker's first bass guitar, the 4000 model, is a typically unusual Rossmeisl design. It has a large body with angular horns, and was the earliest electric bass guitar to feature a scale length (at 33 inches) that was virtually the same as Fender's 34-inch Precision. The 4000 first appeared on Rickenbacker's July 1957 pricelist at $279.50 (which made it $60 more than a Precision).

The Rickenbacker 4000 is also historically interesting as the first bass guitar to be constructed in the 'through-neck' style. This is where the neck is not bolted (like Fender) or glued (like Gibson) to the body, but extends right through the length of the instrument, with 'wings' attached either side to complete the full body shape. A supposed benefit is that the strings and their associated bridge, nut, and tuners are all located on the same piece of wood, enhancing sustain and tonal resonance. More likely, Rickenbacker found this an efficient and straightforward production technique. Rossmeisl had already used it for the company's innovative Combo 400 guitar a year earlier.

Rock'n'roll bass guitar

Despite additions to the bass market in the mid 1950s by makers competing with Fender's Precision, popular use of the electric bass guitar remained scarce at the time. At first, the emerging rock'n'roll music seemed to stay mostly in the hands of slapping double bass players: Marshall Lytle with Bill Haley's Comets ('Rock Around The Clock' hit Number 1 in the U.S.A. in July 1955), Bill Black with Elvis Presley ('Heartbreak Hotel' 1956), Jack Neal with Gene Vincent's Blue Caps ('Be-Bop-A-Lula' 1956), and Joe B. Mauldin with Buddy Holly's Crickets ('That'll Be The Day' 1957).

But changes were underway. Bill Black got a Fender Precision probably in early 1957: photographs reveal one in the MGM studio during the filming of

Jailhouse Rock, and Presley's title track recorded in April sounds like Black is using his new Fender.

There are also pictures from around this time of Black using a Precision on-stage. But he continued to play a lot of double bass and didn't immediately warm to the new electric. At a session a few days after 'Jailhouse Rock' he threw his Precision across the studio floor and stormed out in frustration, angry at his inability to get down the striking intro for '(You're So Square) Baby I Don't Care'. Apparently Elvis completed the bass part himself.[30]

Marshall Lytle left Bill Haley shortly after the success of 'Rock Around The Clock', although he had switched to Fender bass during 1955 for stage work, continuing with double bass for recording. Joe Mauldin too switched from upright to Precision, making the move in summer 1958 for what turned out to be Buddy Holly's last tours (Waylon Jennings played Fender bass on the final tour in early '59). Fender basses were turning up in other live shows, too, at the time, including the backing bands of Jerry Lee Lewis and B.B. King.

It wasn't only double bass players who were switching to the new Fender. Guitarist Bobby Jones, from Greenville, South Carolina, replaced Jack Neal in Gene Vincent's Blue Caps around April 1957 and always played Fender bass, unlike his predecessor. He'd arrived in the band already with his Fender Precision, which he'd bought a year earlier from his previous bandleader, Greenville radio and TV personality Country Earl.

Jones's first recording session with Vincent was in June 1957 at the famous Capitol Tower studio in Hollywood. "I was told I was the first guy to play electric bass there," he recalls. "We were on our way to the studio, and the road manager says well, you won't get to play with the band, they'll have to have a staff musician play the doghouse bass. I said oh my goodness. Well, we got there and set up anyway and started playing, and the engineer says he's not picking me up well enough, can't I use a pick? I was playing my Precision with my thumb. So I said well yes, I guess I can, and I started using a pick. I never did play like the bass players now, with all their fingers. I played with a pick till the day I quit playing."[31]

It's good that the Capitol studio people allowed Jones to play electric bass, because we can now appreciate his early electric bass on some great Vincent cuts, like 'Lotta Lovin'' from that first session, a Number 13 hit in July '57. Blue Caps drummer Dickie Harrell certainly noticed the arrival of Jones's rounder, fuller electric sound and, on this one, his prominent walking runs under the two guitar solos. "'Lotta Lovin'' was a completely different sound," said Harrell. "The electric adds so much to the music."[32]

■ **Danelectro Long Horn 1958** (above) Danelectro's innovations included the six-string bass, in effect a guitar tuned an octave lower than usual. Duane Eddy was its best known player and this example belongs to him.

■ **Fender VI 1962** (main bass) From its onboard vibrato to the tight string-spacing, Fender's 'baritone' six-string bass was clearly aimed at guitarists rather than bass players. However, **Jack Bruce** was an early convert to its charms: he is pictured (right) playing one in 1966 with Cream before he switched to a four-string Gibson EB-3. Fender's VI offered guitarists a bass sound and was tuned an octave lower than a regular guitar. The instrument has remained a specialist item, and six-string basses would become quite different in purpose and design in later years. (The VI shown here is an early version that has a three-switch panel under the pickups; later VIs, from about 1963, have four switches on that panel.)

■ **Danelectro UB-2 1958** (right) Danelectro was set up by Nathan Daniel in New York in 1955. Together with the later and more striking Long Horn model (pictured opposite), Danelectro defined the early idea of the six-string bass. Soundwise, it sat usefully between a conventional four-string bass and a regular six-string guitar. Some studio players at the time found that a six-string bass mixed with a double bass gave an interesting click-and-boom combination, which Nashville producers called 'tic tac bass'.

A few months after Jones joined The Blue Caps, Fender provided the band with guitars and basses and amps – "a lease or whatever, for the publicity" says Jones – but somehow Fender ended up keeping his original '56 Precision. When he left the band in 1958, Jones bought a new Precision, which he used locally until he gave up playing in 1986. It's that bass he recently donated for display at the Rock & Roll Hall Of Fame – but understandably he wishes he still had his '56.

Meanwhile, over in Chicago, guitarist Dave Myers was a member of The Aces, a hot blues band that included harp man Little Walter. While his brother Louis played lead, Dave played bassy guitar. That's probably him at the bottom of the sweaty, distorted howl of Walter's 1954 Checker cut 'You Better Watch Yourself'. It's hard to imagine how an acoustic instrument could have made it in those circumstances.

Myers switched to a Fender Precision in 1958 and played it on sessions and gigs with bluesmen like Otis Rush and Earl Hooker. Rush claimed it was he who persuaded Myers to buy a Fender bass. "I went to St. Louis, where Ike Turner had this Fender bass. There wasn't no Fender bass in Chicago," said Rush.[33] Another claimant to the title for first electric bass in the blues world is Homesick James, who sounds like he might be using a Fender on Elmore James's '12 Year Old Boy', recorded in Chicago in 1957.

Gradually, bassists were beginning to see the electric bass as the natural instrument for rock and related music. Guybo Smith added a trebly bass-guitar contribution to Eddie Cochran's 'Summertime Blues' hit of August 1958, while in the U.K. Brian Gregg created a pleasing throb below Johnny Kidd & The Pirates' raucous 'Shakin All Over' (1960). A rash of instrumental pop tunes began to feature players like Nokie Edwards (on The Ventures' 'Walk – Don't Run', 1960) and Jet Harris (on The Shadows' 'Apache', also 1960) who underlined the bass guitar's role as the natural, equal partner to the lead and rhythm guitars in these new pop groups.

Duane Eddy's instrumental hit 'Rebel Rouser', recorded in March 1958, featured two bass players: Jimmy Simmons on double bass, to give depth and tone to the bassline, and Buddy Wheeler playing the same notes on electric bass guitar, adding a percussive, attacking edge. This was what Eddy's producer Lee Hazlewood called 'click bass'. It's a technique that turned up on other records made around the time, notably in Nashville where it was termed 'tic tac bass'.

Presley's 'Stuck On You' (March 1960) has Bob Moore on double bass and session guitarist Hank Garland on six-string electric bass, while Patsy Cline's 'I Fall To Pieces' (November 1960) features the tireless Moore on double bass and Harold Bradley on Danelectro six-string bass. The first decent British rock'n'roll album, Billy Fury's *The Sound Of Fury* (May 1960), features Bill Stark on double bass and Alan Weighell on bass guitar. German easy-listening king Bert Kaempfert's many hits began with the November 1960 single 'Wunderland Bei Nacht', which has more clicky two-bass work with Kuddel Greve on double bass and Ladi Geisler on bass guitar.

As the 1960s began, at last the attractions of the electric bass were dawning on musicians. It was portable, it made it relatively easier to play complicated lines, it was more straightforward to record, and it added a powerful new element to the sound of any band.

Defining the Precision

Back at the Fender company, despite the exciting new development of their solidbody electric bass, their main business during a good deal of the 1950s remained in amplifiers and electric steel guitars. These were vitally important to the reorganised Fender operation – with new buildings and a new sales operation headed by Don Randall – and they rapidly expanded the lines. In the years following the introduction of the Stratocaster guitar in 1954, the company's fortunes were beginning to turn around. Gradually it seemed as if the Precision, Telecaster, and Stratocaster would also become important to the company's business in the coming years.

Fender made changes to the design of the Precision Bass in 1954 and 1957, indicating that they were still searching for a combination of features that would attract musicians. In 1954, the team simply contoured the body (replacing the original slab style), made sunburst the standard colour, and swapped the black pickguard for a white one. But the final alterations of 1957 – new pickup and bridge, larger headstock, different pickguard with integrated controls – defined the look of the Precision Bass for decades to come. Fender knew from the cool Stratocaster guitar that they could make the P-Bass look better and slicker, and they proudly showed off the new-style bass to the trade at the summer '57 NAMM convention in Chicago.

Leo Fender explained later to several interviewers that, in the 1950s, Fender never emphasised the humbucking capabilities of their pickups because their patent attorney had told them that a pickup of this type had been patented back in the 1930s. Leo also said that humbuckers were introduced on the company's basses because he considered the original single-coil type of pickup too hard on the amplifier's loudspeakers, whereas the humbucking types offered a softer, less spiky signal, no doubt easing the workload on Fender's amp-repair department.

■ **Rickenbacker 4001S 1964** After the original 4000 model, Rickenbacker issued this upgrade in 1961. The 4001S soon became very successful in the hands of bassists such as Paul McCartney of The Beatles and Chris Squire of Yes. The new model had a revised bridge and redesigned pickguard, an extra pickup in addition to the original 'horseshoe' unit, and a set of more sophisticated controls.

■ Rickenbacker's distinctive bass was designed by Roger Rossmeisl, a German guitar-maker who came to the California company in 1954. A promo shot (right) for the 4000 bass adds a glamorous touch.

**■ Rickenbacker 4000
1957** (main bass) First-year example of Rickenbacker's debut bass guitar, this one owned by Van Halen bass man Michael Anthony.

■ While Rickenbacker toyed with the idea of a bass guitar, their fellow Californians at Fender saw more players beginning to adopt the Fender Precision Bass, especially younger rock'n'roll players who discovered the punch and dynamism an electric bass could add to a band. A few examples here show what was going on.

Bobby Jones (top, far left) uses a Precision to supply the deep notes for Gene Vincent's Blue Caps at Capitol studio in Hollywood in 1957. In the same year, Elvis's bass man **Bill Black** (hidden behind that singer, left), who had started out playing double bass with Presley, shifted to a Precision, just visible in this rare shot.

Leo's patent for the new Precision 'split' pickup (filed January 1959 and issued March 28th 1961) provided more detail. First, however, they described the current bass scene. "Electric guitars of the bass type have, in recent years, been coming into use as a replacement for the very large and clumsy string basses conventionally employed. Such bass guitars are sufficiently small to be held on the lap of a seated guitarist, and require relatively little transportation and storage space. Furthermore, such guitars are much simpler and less strenuous to play than conventional non-electric string basses."

The pickup patent continued: "In order to achieve the necessary low pitch, the guitar strings must be much more bulky and massive than those of a standard guitar. Furthermore, the excursion of each string on both sides of the neutral position, resulting from each plucking or picking action, is greater than that of a string of a standard guitar. These and other factors have made it exceedingly difficult to provide an electro-magnetic pickup construction which will properly convert the string vibration into electrical impulses, and which may be adequately adjusted to the various strings in order to achieve the desired volume relationships."[34]

Fender's 'split' humbucking pickup did much to solve these problems: the position of the pickup units relative to the strings was fully adjustable; electrical interference hum was effectively cancelled; and the vibrations of the strings were more accurately sensed.

The Precision's bridge, also new on the revised 1957 model, disposed of the two-strings-per-saddle compromise of the original version and offered a saddle for each string.

Fender's press release said: "This [is] an entirely new type [of] mechanical bridge for individual string adjustments. The player can achieve any desired string action with this new unit. The four [saddles] are readily accessible and adjustments can be easily made by the player."[35]

Don Randall recalls that one of the reasons for enlarging the headstock on the new Precision concerned a shortcoming of the original design. "We had a problem with a deadspot on the first string, around the seventh fret. A lot of people never found that out," he laughs, "but some of the better bass players did. We worked to try to overcome that, and enlarging the headstock helped some. I think we determined that the resonance of the body, neck, and head with the seventh fret position acted like a shock absorber; it kind of snubbed the tone. The mass of the body and of the head and the stiffness of the neck all had an effect on the problem, but we never did solve it completely."[36]

The revised Precision appeared on the cover of Fender's 1957–58 catalogue, their first with a colour cover, which opened out to reveal a new-design sunburst P-Bass among the other instruments on display. It was on the March 1958 pricelist at $219.50 (which would have the same buying power as about $1,500 of today's money).

Around 1959, Fender changed the Precision Bass to have a rosewood fingerboard, in contrast to earlier P-basses with their frets laid directly into the face of the maple neck. Some players like the smooth, almost slippery feel of maple, while others prefer the more textured touch of rosewood. Maple remained as an option at various times following the introduction of rosewood.

Good enough for Jazz

Despite the slowly growing awareness of bass guitars among players, all the signs were that guitar companies still regarded the electric bass with caution by the time the 1960s started. Harmony, a very big Chicago-based musical instrument company, were not at all slow in identifying and exploiting market opportunities – and they did not offer a bass guitar until 1962, with the launch of their H-22 model. Similarly, Fender did not feel that the market would support a second model in their bass range until 1960.

In the same way that they had introduced the Stratocaster as a refined high-end companion for the Telecaster, Fender decided to add a new model above the Precision Bass. It was the Jazz Bass, which the factory started to produce in March 1960. In June, Fender Sales showed it to the music trade in Rooms 894 and 895 at the Palmer House during the summer NAMM show in Chicago. The instrument first appeared on the July pricelist at $279.50 in regular sunburst, alongside the Precision.

Those two lone basses were in stark contrast to the rest of the company's rapidly growing product lines. That July '60 pricelist included 13 amplifiers (Bandmaster, Bassman, Champ, Concert, Deluxe, Harvard, Princeton, Pro Amp, Super, Tremolux, Twin Amp, Vibrasonic, Vibrolux), seven electric steel guitars (Champ, Deluxe, Dual, Stringmaster, Studio Deluxe, 400, 1000), and six regular electric guitars (Duo-Sonic, Esquire, Jazzmaster, Musicmaster, Stratocaster, Telecaster).

"We were always market driven," explains Don Randall, who was the boss at Fender Sales. "After establishing the fact that bass guitars would sell and that people wanted them, then the next thing was to make a prettier one, a more elaborate one. We wanted an upscale model to put on the market. The Jazz Bass wasn't Leo's idea particularly, it was more of a marketing idea, something that we wanted in order to expand the line. Mostly it was not just a love of the

the
best
things
don't
always
need
big
packages

Proof . . . the popular Fender precision bass. It's the instrument with the revolutionary concept . . . designed to offer the highest level of bassmanship yet possible. Conveniently smaller in size and easier to play, this sensational instrument provides the tone range and musical quality suited to every type of instrumentation, combo to full orchestra. Bassmen agree its fast-action neck improves technique and inspires a whole new concept of bass playing.

Why not visit your leading music dealer and ask to hear this remarkable instrument yourself.

Fender SALES INC
308 E. 5th ST. • SANTA ANA, CALIF.

INTERNATIONAL MUSICIAN

■ Fender grew confident about their new bass guitars, boasting in this clever 1957 ad (above) that they "inspire a whole new concept of bass playing".

■ **Fender Precision Bass 1957** (main bass, above) The final revision came in '57, as a two-piece humbucker replaced the earlier single-coil 'bar' and the headstock became wider. Fender briefly used a new gold-coloured anodised pickguard. Now, collectors consider this combination of 50s features – contoured body, one-piece maple neck, split pickup, anodised 'guard – as the most desirable on an early Precision. This lovely example is owned by Bob Daisley, best known for his work with Ozzy Osbourne.

■ Illustrating a key difference between an early-50s and late-50s Precision, the two side views (right) show a slab-body 1951 bass and the contoured '57 version. Into the 60s, and groups started to focus on the power of the two-guitars/bass/drums line-up, as with top US instro outfit The Ventures (left). **Bob Bogle** and his '57-style P-Bass are the centre of attention here.

■ **Fender Precision Bass 1955** Fender's first changes to the original 1951 Precision came with this version in '54. Most obvious for the musician was the way the body was contoured on the revision, making for a more comfortable playing experience. Visuals changed too: the finish was now sunburst and the pickguard was white.

product: it was a market-oriented move."[37] Market-driven or not, the new Jazz Bass was a brilliant addition to the Fender line, and must have seemed at the time to be an interesting new alternative to the Precision, at the very least.

Compared to the Precision, the Jazz is a little more sizeable and has a different feel and sound, with the design distinguished by an offset-waist body that was similar in style to the Jazzmaster guitar that Fender had launched two years earlier. The Jazz Bass also differed from the Precision in its narrow string-spacing at the nut, which gave the neck a distinctly tapered feel, and its provision of two pickups, linked in humbucking mode like the split pickup of the revised Precision but offering a wider tonal range.

The Jazz and Precision would, of course, go on to become the mighty twin peaks of Fender's electric bass success. As time went on, some Fender players preferred the out-and-out simplicity and grainy bottom-end growl of the Precision, while other bassists felt more inclined to the crisper tones and the different neck feel of the Jazz.

At first the Jazz came with what Fender called "tandem volume and tone controls" using dual-concentric pots, which we now call the stack-knob layout. This offered a tone control on top and a volume control underneath each 'stack', for each pickup. This was changed a couple of years later to a three-control layout, with two larger knobs for volume per pickup and a smaller overall tone control. Fender also took the opportunity around '62 to remove the messy body-mounted string mutes, which almost no one used.

And now in (custom) colour

One of the earliest pieces of publicity for Fender's Custom Color finishes had come in the April 1957 issue of an instruments trade magazine. Don Randall, according to the report, "recently revealed the availability of the Fender Precision Bass in custom Du Pont Duco finish in addition to the blonde and regular sunburst finishes". Randall told the reporter that the Precision had found "rapidly increasing acceptance among bass players throughout the country and is now included in the instrumentation of many of the nation's top musical organizations".[38]

Most Fenders of the early years came only in standard finishes: blond (pale yellow) for Precisions, Telecasters, and Esquires, and then yellow-to-brown sunburst from '54 for Precisions and Strats. By 1956, 'player's choice' solid-colour guitars became an option. During the following year, these Du Pont paint finishes were in Fender's catalogues as 'custom colors', a name that has stuck ever since.

By the early 1960s, Fender had come up with a defined list of their officially available Custom Colors and issued special colour charts that were intended to publicise and help customers select the various shades.

The original 1961 chart featured Black, Burgundy Mist Metallic, Dakota Red, Daphne Blue, Fiesta Red, Foam Green, Inca Silver Metallic, Lake Placid Blue Metallic, Olympic White, Shell Pink, Sherwood Green Metallic, Shoreline Gold Metallic, Sonic Blue, and Surf Green.

The second Fender colour chart, in '63, lost Shell Pink and gained Candy Apple Red Metallic. The third, in 1965, lost Burgundy Mist Metallic, Daphne Blue, Inca Silver Metallic, Sherwood Green Metallic, Shoreline Gold Metallic, and Surf Green, and gained – all Metallics – Blue Ice, Charcoal Frost, Firemist Gold, Firemist Silver, Ocean Turquoise, and Teal Green.

The car industry was having a marked effect on some American guitar manufacturers, not least in this ability to boost the look of an already stylish object with a rich, sparkling paint job. Du Pont was the biggest supplier of paint to the auto factories, notably General Motors. Fender used paints from Du Pont's Duco nitro-cellulose lines, such as Fiesta Red or Foam Green, as well as the more colour-retentive Lucite acrylics like Lake Placid Blue Metallic or Burgundy Mist Metallic.

In fact, the names Fender gave to the colours usually came from the original car makers' terms: Fiesta Red, for example, was first used by Ford in 1956 on its Thunderbird model, while Lake Placid Blue originally appeared on a 1958 Cadillac Brougham. Candy Apple Red, however, was unusual in that it was a Fender original and not a car colour.[39]

George Fullerton remembered going out to a local paint store probably in 1957, buying a Fiesta Red mix, and then returning to the factory and applying it to a guitar body. He said this experiment was what started Fender's defined Custom Color line. "That first one became Fiesta Red," recalled Fullerton. "The Du Pont company made that colour and you could buy it right across the counter. That should have been a patent, that colour, but who knows at the time you do a thing? Meanwhile, the sales office and Don Randall laughed at it, said who in hell wants a coloured guitar, specially a red one."[40]

Decades later, the basses bearing these original Fiesta Reds, Sonic Blues, Burgundy Mists and the like have become prime collectables. Many collectors rate a Custom Color Fender, especially an early one, as an essential catch.

The colours didn't add much to the price, originally. In 1961, for example, a Custom Color (including blond) would add just $11.47 extra on top of a regular sunburst $229.50 Precision Bass and $13.97 extra to a $279.50 Jazz Bass. In

■ **Fender Jazz Bass 1964**
(right) Here's the regular
three-knob Jazz in splendid
teal green custom colour.
The catalogue (above)
features the earlier 'stack
knob' version alongside a
couple of Precisions. A clip
from a '65 brochure
(opposite) details key
features of the Jazz. **Joe
Osborn** (left) was a busy
studio musician who often
took out his Jazz Bass to
create fine basslines for
many artists, including The
Mamas & The Papas,
Simon & Garfunkel, and
The Carpenters.

■ **Fender Jazz Bass 1960**
(main bass) New this year, the Jazz has two pickups that give a wider tonal range than the Precision. The narrower neck also provides players with a different feel. At first, the Jazz was fitted with two 'dual concentric' volume and tone controls (known as stack knobs), as on this sunburst example. These early models also had 'slab' fingerboards, with a straight join between board and neck, which changed in 1962 to a curved join.

■ **Harmony H-22 1963**
(below) During the 1960s, Harmony of Chicago was the biggest US producer of guitars. Significantly, they did not think it worth issuing a bass guitar until 1962, the result being this bass, typical of their varied output. Steve Winwood's bassist brother Muff used one in Britain in The Spencer Davis Group during the 1960s.

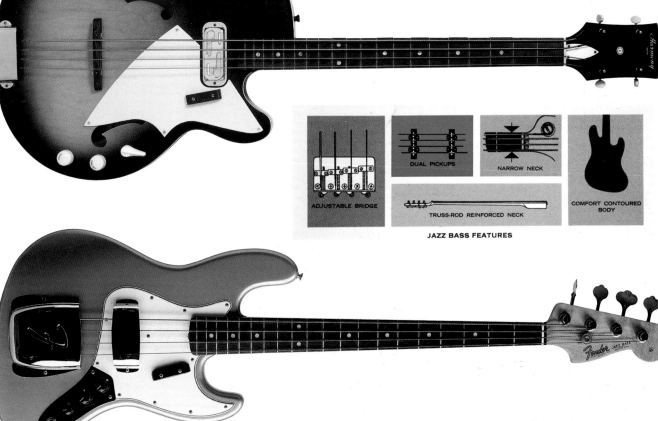

ADJUSTABLE BRIDGE

DUAL PICKUPS

NARROW NECK

TRUSS-ROD REINFORCED NECK

COMFORT CONTOURED BODY

JAZZ BASS FEATURES

today's collector market, the price differential between an original regular-finish instrument and one in a genuine Custom Color has become much greater. This is despite the prevalence of 're-finished' basses, some of which are now so accurate that even alleged experts can be fooled into declaring a fake finish as original. Just how much is a coat of paint worth?

Paul and the violin bass

Pop music exploded in popularity as the 1960s got underway, and demand for electric basses boomed. In 1963, Johnny Cymbal had a hit with 'Mr. Bass Man' where he sang: "Hey, Mister Bass Man, you're the hidden king of rock'n'roll." He meant a doo-wop bass vocalist. But he might just as well have been singing about the electric bass revolution.

The bass guitar was accepted as an essential part of the studio and stage line-ups of the new pop groups. Nobody did more to fuel this demand than The Beatles, who from 1964 became, quite simply, the most popular and visible group in the world. They had self-contained playing and composing skills and established the quartet personnel of two guitars, bass guitar, and drums. Paul McCartney, born in Liverpool in 1942, started out as a guitarist but became The Beatles' bassman when their first bassist decided he was a better artist than a musician and left the group.

McCartney explains: "Stu Sutcliffe was a friend of John Lennon's, they were at art school together, and Stu had won a painting competition. The prize was 75 quid. We said to him: That's exactly the price of a Hofner bass. He said it's supposed to be for painting materials, but we managed to persuade him over a cappuccino. It kind of dwarfed him a bit, the [large-body] Hofner – he was a smallish guy – but it looked kind of heroic. He stood a certain way; he had shades; he looked the part."

Some people, McCartney included, have said that Sutcliffe wasn't much good as a player but he did at least look the part with his Hofner 500/5; others say he was no better or worse than the rest. "None of us wanted to be the bass player," says McCartney. "It wasn't the number one job – we wanted to be up front. In our minds it was the fat guy in the group nearly always played the bass, and he stood at the back. None of us wanted that. We wanted to be up front singing, looking good, to pull the birds."

The Beatles landed a second gruelling season of gigs in Hamburg, Germany, in mid 1961. Sutcliffe decided to stay there with a girlfriend and be a painter. "So it was like oh-oh, we haven't got a bass player," says McCartney. "And everyone sort of turned round and looked at me. I was a bit lumbered with it, really; it was like well – it'd better be you, then. I don't think you would have caught John doing it, he would have said: 'No, you're kidding, I've got a nice new Rickenbacker!' I didn't have a guitar at the time – it had been smashed up and I was playing piano on stage then – so I couldn't really say that I wanted to be a guitarist. So, eventually, I found a little shop in the centre of Hamburg, and I saw this violin-shaped bass guitar in the window, the Hofner."[41]

It was a Hofner 500/1, a German-made hollowbody similar to Gibson's Electric Bass model and generally referred to since as a 'violin bass'. McCartney, a left-hander, acquired his first Hofner in 1961 and bought it for the equivalent of around £30 (about $65 then). The Steinway store in Hamburg ordered the unusual left-handed model specially for McCartney. He got a second 500/1 around September 1963 and stuck to this model as his sole Beatles live-performance bass and his main bass in the recording studio until 1965 (although he pulled it out again for the '69 *Let It Be* sessions).

Karl Hofner started his company back in the 1880s in Schoenbach, Germany, at first making violins, cellos, and double basses. Hofner guitars appeared in 1925, by which time Karl's sons Josef and Walter had joined their father, and the business grew rapidly.

After World War II, the Hofner family moved to Erlangen and began production again in 1949, two years later relocating to Bubenreuth. Archtop guitars were added to the catalogue during the early 1950s with electrics following soon after, and the 500/1 was the company's first bass, introduced in 1956. Various reissues of the 500/1 have appeared in more recent years.

Given the way that the electric bass was quickly establishing itself as pop music's replacement for the double bass, it's surprising to look back and realise that McCartney and the Hofner 500/1 – now one of the best known images of player and bass – looked a little like a musician with a miniature double bass around his neck.

James and the Motown beat

On the other side of the Atlantic, a player from a different background began to make a mark. James Jamerson was born in South Carolina in 1936 and moved with his family to Detroit, Michigan, in 1951. At 18, Jamerson started to play double bass, with jazz ambitions, but in 1959 he began to play sessions for a record company in Detroit owned by Berry Gordy. That company would soon be known throughout the world as Motown.

With remarkable foresight, Gordy christened his company of black musicians 'The Sound of Young America'. Motown's fresh merger of pop and

■ Fender's 1966–67 catalogue (right) had the upstanding sunburst line (Jazz, Bass V, Precision) with a couple of nice custom colour examples: a fiesta red Precision (on the stool) and a firemist silver Jazz (on the floor). Fender began offering colours in the 1950s but standardised a set of 'custom colors' later that decade, based on the range of paints made for cars by DuPont. They are now very collectable.

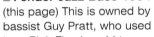

■ **Fender Jazz Bass 1964** (this page) This is owned by bassist Guy Pratt, who used it on Pink Floyd world tours and other dates. The fine Fender custom colour that remains on this careworn instrument is burgundy mist metallic. (The pickups are 'active' EMGs, replacing the originals, a popular move among some players who seek a more modern tone than 60s pickups offer.)

coats of many colours

CUSTOM FINISHES FOR *Fender* FINE ELECTRIC INSTRUMENTS

These 14 Colors, plus Blond, Available at 5% Additional cost
Sunburst Finishes Standard at no Extra cost

LAKE PLACID BLUE METALLIC	SHERWOOD GREEN METALLIC	
LUCITE 2876-L		DUCO 2576-M
DAPHNE BLUE	FOAM GREEN	
DUCO 2804		DUCO 2253
SONIC BLUE		
DUCO 2295		
SHORELINE GOLD METALLIC	SURF GREEN	
LUCITE 2939-L		DUCO 2461
OLYMPIC WHITE	INCA SILVER METALLIC	
LUCITE 2818-L		LUCITE 2936-L
	FIESTA RED	
		DUCO 2015-M
BURGUNDY MIST METALLIC	DAKOTA RED	
LUCITE 2936-L		DUCO 2509-M
BLACK	SHELL PINK	
DUCO 1711-X		DUCO 2371

Not Available for Duo-Sonic and Music master
Colors Subject to Change Without Notice

■ **Fender Precision Bass 1963** (far left); **Fender Jazz Bass 1966** (left) Two more luscious custom colours: the Precision is finished in lake placid blue, the Jazz, by this time with 'block' markers, in candy apple red. Fender issued charts to help customers select a colour; this one (above) dates from the early 60s and includes foam green, sonic blue, shell pink, and dakota red.

■ **Fender Precision Bass 1966** Fender was bought by CBS in 1965, and instruments made afterward are known as post-CBS. This is an ex-John Entwistle bass and a good example of how a custom colour can add a touch of class to an already desirable Fender. This one is finished in firemist gold, a colour name that came into use at Fender around 1965.

43

R&B from artists such as The Supremes, The Four Tops, Smokey Robinson, Marvin Gaye, and Stevie Wonder did indeed become the sound of young America – and well beyond – attracting a huge audience of black as well as white fans during the label's heyday in the mid to late 1960s.

James Jamerson switched to electric bass in 1961, buying a Fender Precision when Gordy asked him to go on the road with Jackie Wilson. After a few changes following the theft of various instruments, Jamerson settled on a 1962 sunburst Precision. From '64, Gordy moved Jamerson from road duties to become a full-time member of Motown's team of studio musicians, unofficially known as The Funk Brothers.

Lamont Dozier was one third of the great Motown production team of Holland-Dozier-Holland. Used to seeing Jamerson playing around town and on early Motown sessions playing double bass, he recalls the bassman turning up to a session with his Fender electric. "I said: What the hell is that, man? I felt like a pioneer or something. I said this ain't no time to experiment, I gotta cut an important song today. He said no man, this is it. He had his Fender. I was shocked at the sound. But he could manoeuvre it."[42]

He certainly could manoeuvre it. The Precision's string mutes were very much part of Jamerson's sound, pressed hard against the strings to give a staccato sound. Jamerson set his heavy-gauge flatwound strings with a very high action and often played with his index finger only – what he called 'the hook'. "Musicians who had the chance to try out his bass usually found it to be almost unplayable," wrote Jamerson's biographer, Allan Slutsky. "But for James it was fine because of his unusual hand strength."[43]

One of the earliest signs of the brilliance to come from Jamerson can be heard in basic form on Marvin Gaye's late-1964 single 'How Sweet It Is (To Be Loved By You)'. After that, Jamerson would shine out on many Detroit-cut Motown hits, including 'Stop! In The Name Of Love' and 'You Keep Me Hangin' On' by The Supremes (1965 and '66), 'Reach Out I'll Be There' and 'Bernadette' by The Four Tops (1966 and '67), and Stevie Wonder's 'I Was Made To Love Her' and 'For Once In My Life' (1967 and '68), among many others. From the later period, the sheer beauty of Jamerson's part on Marvin Gaye's 'What's Going On' (recorded 1970) is an unmissable treat. The *What's Going On* album, released in 1971 with Jamerson on all but two tracks, was the first major Motown record to provide musician credits.

Jamerson's powerfully rhythmic basslines were melodic, syncopated pieces of magic. His recorded grooves with Motown helped to change the perception of the electric bass guitar's role from the root-note machine of pop music and the rarely challenged root-and-fifth routine of country to become an important part of the overall musical picture. He played with Motown until 1972 and died at the age of just 47, in 1983, following alcohol-related problems and ill health.

Beatle bass magic

Back in England in the early 1960s, Paul McCartney was one of many players who heard the wonderful Motown bass work and noted the beautiful lines and musical invention. Not that anybody knew that the man they heard in the grooves was Jamerson.

"As time went on," recalls McCartney, "James Jamerson became my hero, although I didn't actually know his name until quite recently. Jamerson and later Brian Wilson of The Beach Boys were my two biggest influences: James because he was so good and melodic, and Brian because he went to very unusual places." It was around this time that Wilson in fact started to use session bassists for Beach Boys records, including Carol Kaye and Ray Pohlman. Listen for Kaye's exceptional work on 'Good Vibrations' (1966), for example.

McCartney himself was hardly inhabiting everyday bass worlds as the 1960s progressed. Gradually his basslines became more melodic and structured and were pushed further forward in the Beatles mix. He'd acquired a Rickenbacker 4001S on The Beatles' August 1965 U.S. tour. Rickenbacker in California used the general design and through-neck construction of their earlier 4000 bass for many subsequent models, including the fancier two-pickup 4001 (1961) and the export version with dot markers, the 4001S (1964).

McCartney started using his new Rick in the studio during October and November 1965 to record songs for the group's *Rubber Soul* album. From that point on he would alternate between the Rickenbacker and his trusty Hofner, creating such recorded bass highlights as the funky scurry of 'The Word', the lazy groove of 'I'm Only Sleeping', or the astonishing full-on joy of 'Rain'.

By the time he recorded the remarkable bass parts for the *Sgt Pepper* LP at the end of 1966 and into 1967, McCartney was using the Rickenbacker as his main studio instrument.

McCartney remembers that he started to experiment with his basslines, moving away from the simpler efforts of earlier recordings based on the root notes of chord sequences. "I wondered what else could you do, how much further could you take it. *Sgt Pepper* ended up being my strongest thing on bass, the independent melodies. On 'Lucy In The Sky With Diamonds', for example, you could easily have had root notes, whereas I was running an independent melody through it, and that became my thing. So once I got over the fact that I

■ **Hofner 500/1 1963** (left-handed bass, below) This German 'violin bass' belongs to Paul McCartney and was the second Hofner bass that the Beatle acquired. He bought his first, with 'close together' pickups, in Hamburg in 1961. The left-handed McCartney received the pictured bass in 1963 and used it on many Beatles recordings and concerts, including the group's last show in San Francisco in '66. This candid shot from summer 1963 (left), snapped backstage at a TV studio, has **Paul McCartney** and **John Lennon** fooling around with both of Paul's 'violin' basses: the '63 bass on the left and the earlier '61 model on the right.

PLAYER OF THE MONTH

"The 'Fiddle Bass' Sound is GREAT" –says PAUL

When Paul McCartney says the Hofner Violin Bass is just Great, you bet it's worth havin' I. That's why SELMER take every one the manufacturer can produce and rush them out to the dealers.

Make a bee line for your nearest Selmer stockist now and see this masterpiece . . . easily the most popular and widely used bass guitar today. Has double-pole, double-coil NOVA-SONIC pick-ups and flick-action switches for instant tone change. Only 55 Guineas. Rich felt-lined Case, 8 Guineas.

Send NOW for free Guitar Brochure

Selmer

NAME
ADDRESS

114 CHARING CROSS ROAD, LONDON, W.C.2.

■ Hofner's UK agent Selmer made a deal with Beatles manager Brian Epstein in 1964 to promote Hofners using **Paul McCartney**'s image. The bassist had already appeared in British magazines wth his bass (like this one, far left), but the Selmer deal resulted in ads (left) and a 'swing tag' fixed to new Hofner instruments in music stores. The tag had a picture of McCartney and the line: "Wishing you every succes with this guitar." These were all early examples of artist endorsement in the new world of pop music.

■ **Hofner 500/1 1956**
Hofner was set up in Germany in the 1880s, and by the 1950s the company was making electric guitars and basses. The 500/1 bass model was their first, appearing in 1956. The body shape was copied from Gibson's EB-1; both are often known as 'violin' basses. This rare early 500/1 has an oval control panel and a body logo.

was lumbered with bass, I did get quite proud to be a bass player. It was all very exciting."[44] Later albums saw McCartney continue to produce the goods, including bass gems such as 'Dear Prudence' on *The White Album*, 'Hey Bulldog' on *Yellow Submarine*, and his bass masterpiece, 'Something' from *Abbey Road*.

Fender gave the band some instruments and gear in 1968, and McCartney may have used a Jazz Bass here and there on the *White Album*, while Lennon or Harrison would sometimes pick up a Bass VI. But it's McCartney's work on Hofner and Rickenbacker throughout the classic recordings of The Beatles that will remain forever as a self-contained and completely convincing masterclass for any aspiring pop bassist.

The sound of the bass guitar in the studio was certainly developing. But how did record fans hear it at the time? Even if there was bass-end there in the first place, it would not have been clearly audible to many of them. When listeners placed their vinyl record on to a small, portable record player and dropped the needle into the groove, the bass player's sound would at best have been a dull, indistinct blur in the tiny speaker. It was the same when they listened to music on small transistor radios – not exactly a bass-heavy experience.

Some engineers were told to limit the amount of bass-end on a record by compressing the sound when they recorded it and reducing the level as they cut masters. They were given no choice: if there was too much bass, there was a danger that the needle would jump right out of a record's groove. It was only further into the 1960s and on into the following decade, as engineers learned the value of bass and discerning listeners bought proper hi-fi systems to play stereo records, that the full joy of the bass guitar's sound and impact became apparent on records.

But as the 1960s progressed, well over ten years after Fender's Precision had first appeared, the electric bass was at last becoming established as *the* modern bass instrument. In their different ways, Paul McCartney and James Jamerson personified this new acceptance. McCartney was an unschooled pop musician, originally a guitarist who was 'lumbered' with the bass but quickly made the instrument his own and showed it off to the world. Jamerson came from a jazz background playing double bass but began to find that pop studio work with his electric bass was far more lucrative – and soon he discovered that he could make beautifully expressive music on bass guitar. His work demonstrated to many session players that the electric bass was a legitimate musical instrument.

Fender too was on a roll, and in the mid 1960s 'Fender Bass' became a generic expression, synonymous with electric bass guitar. In the 1965 American

Federation of Musicians' directory of union members in Local 47 (Los Angeles), for example, there were three headings for bass guitarists: 'Electric Bass', 'Bass Guitar', and 'Fender Bass'. The 'Fender Bass' listing was the longest and included a good number of active L.A. session musicians.

Fender for sale, one previous owner

In January 1965, Fender was sold to CBS (Columbia Broadcasting System) for $13 million and became the Fender Musical Instruments division of Columbia Records Distribution Corporation. According to some insiders, the problem with CBS was that they seemed to think it enough simply to pour money into Fender. Sales did increase and profits did go up – Don Randall said income almost doubled in the first year that CBS owned Fender. Profit became paramount, said Forrest White. Output increased dramatically, but as a result quality gradually went down into the 1970s. The original team that had built up Fender grew disenchanted and one by one left the new organisation.

Fender salesman Dale Hyatt was fielding complaints from store owners. He reckoned the factory's quality stayed relatively stable until around 1968 and then declined. "They got very sloppy with the finish, and the neck sockets were being cut way over size. They created their own competition, letting the door wide open for everybody else, including the Japanese."[45]

CBS made some cosmetic changes to various Fender models. In the bass line, the major visual change was to the Jazz Bass, which in 1965 gained binding on the fingerboard and, the following year, shifted from dot-shape position markers to blocks. Generally, CBS seemed to be fiddling for fiddling's sake.

In 1966, CBS completed the construction of a new $1.3 million Fender factory, which had been planned before they purchased the company. It was right next to Fender's existing buildings on the South Raymond site. The new owners were well set for a big push on production – and CBS didn't have much cause for concern in terms of demand. Pop music was, of course, flourishing in the 1960s – and Fenders were everywhere.

The Precision and Jazz were superb Fender mainstays, but the new models that did show up – the Bass V (1965), the Mustang Bass (1966), and the Telecaster Bass (1968) – did little to expand or enhance Fender's influence beyond the company's leading bass duo.

The Bass V was quite different from our modern idea of a five-string bass. It had a short 15-fret fingerboard and the extra string was a high one, tuned to C. It effectively took the same musical range as the four-string 20-fret Fender, from low E to high E-flat, but condensed it across five strings and 15 frets. It

■ **Rickenbacker 4001S 1964** (main bass) This belongs to Paul McCartney. It was given to him by Rickenbacker during a Beatles US tour in 1965, and he used it on many Beatle records. Originally it was in fireglo red finish but can be seen with a suitably psychedelic refinish in the Magical Mystery Tour film. Paul used it later on Wings tours and recordings (see below), by which time he had stripped the paint down to the natural wood and reshaped the body horn.

■ **Paul McCartney** continued to use his Rickenbacker bass in Wings; he's pictured with it (above) in the studio in 1973. During the 60s, British bass players used instruments from a variety of sources. The US-made hollowbody Epiphone Rivoli was popular with some, including **Chas Chandler** with The Animals (above left). **Bill Wyman** of The Rolling Stones bought his German-made Framus Star Bass (ad, opposite) in 1963, around the time of the group's first single, and while he was seen with it on gigs and TV dates, he often preferred his own homemade fretless bass in the studio.

■ Great Motown session bassist **James Jamerson** (below) is pictured here with drummer Earl Van Dyke. Fender issued a replica **Jamerson Tribute Precision** (opposite) in the early 90s.

may be that it was designed to allow bassists reading music to reach upper notes across the fingerboard without moving playing position. But the Bass V never caught on, and it would fade from the line by 1970.

The Mustang was a budget-price model and Fender's first short-scale bass. The Telecaster Bass followed the general style of the original pre-1957 single-coil Precision Bass, copying its maple neck, slim headstock, and the shape of its pickguard and control panel. Its release was a very significant event – not so much for the instrument itself, but because it marked the first time that Fender reissued an earlier design.

William Johnson, CBS's marketing director, said in 1968 that the original had been "developed almost 20 years ago. At the time, too few appreciated it, so it was dropped from the line. More recently it has been rediscovered by pros and veterans in the music field. We were receiving reports that musicians were searching for this instrument in music stores everywhere. After an industry-wide study, we decided to reintroduce the instrument and have resumed production, building it as we did a generation ago".[46]

Here in a nutshell is the modern idea of retro – about 30 years before it became fashionable. It's a remarkably prescient moment in Fender's history, but sadly this late-1960s version of the idea was ill-conceived and shortlived. Fender changed the Telecaster Bass in 1972 to have a covered humbucker at the neck, meaning this new-look (and equally unsuccessful) Tele Bass had less in common with the original-look Precision. Many more reissues would follow in decades to come, and the re-creation of past glories would become a profitable obsession at Fender. But for now the idea of reissuing classic designs went back on the shelf for some time.

The wild Wildwoods

A firm innovation – for Fender, at least – came in the shape of a new line of hollowbody electrics. These were the first electric-acoustics from Fender, a maker identified in many players' mind as the prime producer of solidbody guitars. Evidently Gibson's EB-2 semi-hollow bass and models by Gretsch and others must have tempted CBS and their search for wider markets.

Leo Fender brought Roger Rossmeisl into the company in 1962 to design acoustic guitars, and Rossmeisl was also responsible for the new electric-acoustic guitars and basses. They were all manufactured at Fender's separate acoustic guitar plant on Missile Way in Fullerton. Rossmeisl, the son of a German guitar-maker, had come to the States in the 1950s and at first worked for Gibson in Michigan, soon moving to Rickenbacker in California where his designs included the classic 4000-series bass style. Rossmeisl's Fender Coronado thinline guitars and two basses – the single-pickup Coronado I (1966) and two-pickup Coronado II (1967) – were the first of his electric designs for Fender.

Despite their conventional double-cutaway bound bodies with large stylised f-holes, they stubbornly employed the standard Fender bolt-on neck and headstock design.

Fender also offered two finish options: a curious dyed Wildwood model described as "truly a happening in sight and sound" with "exciting rainbow hues of greens, blues, and golds"; and a white-to-brown shaded finish called Antigua. Fender's first try with thinline electric-acoustics was not a success. The various versions were all dropped from the line within a few years.

Jack, John, Joe, and jazz

Improvements to stage and studio equipment during the 1960s made the bass guitar increasingly audible, and vital musical steps were taken by players such as Jack Bruce in Cream, Phil Lesh in The Grateful Dead, John Entwistle in The Who, and Jack Casady in Jefferson Airplane, along with studio bassists like Tommy Cogbill (Wilson Pickett, Aretha Franklin, Percy Sledge) and Joe Osborn (Simon & Garfunkel, Mamas & The Papas, Fifth Dimension) in the States, and in Britain future Led Zeppelin anchorman John Paul Jones (Dusty Springfield, Herman's Hermits, Donovan), among many others.

One of the first appearances of electric bass in modern jazz came on Miles Davis's *Filles De Kilimanjaro*, where Ron Carter – normally a staunch double bass man – switched to Fender for a few pieces recorded in summer 1968. But the album that really showed the way forward for electric jazz-rock was Miles's *Bitches Brew* (1969), with Harvey Brooks on bass guitar on some of the tracks.

Thunderbirds are go

Gibson had modified their bass catalogue in 1961 to include the new EB-3 solidbody bass. This was in effect a bass version of Gibson's new SG guitar line, introduced the same year and described as having an "ultra thin, hand contoured, double cutaway body". The new EB bass style must have seemed a radical departure at the time. The body edges looked as if a sculptor had been at work rather than a guitar-maker, resulting in a modernistic mix of bevels and points and angles. Gibson had of course noticed Fender's growing success with its sleek pair of revised Precision and new Jazz.

The EB-3 had that mahogany body, two humbucking pickups (larger at neck, smaller at the bridge), a four-position tone switch (but no pickup selector), a

**■ Fender Telecaster Bass
1968** (this page, centre)
This was Fender's first
'reissue' of an old model.
When launched in 1968, it
tried to be like the original
Precision: small head,
maple neck, single pickup,
simple controls. It didn't
succeed, but Fender would
return to the idea. This one
is owned by Cocteau Twin
Robin Guthrie.

**■ Fender Mustang Bass
1969** (right) After Fender
was taken over by CBS in
1965 the company's
marketing strategy
changed. The Mustang,
offered from 1966, was
Fender's first short-scale
bass, aimed to be more
accessible for the new
generation of guitarists now
also playing bass. The
pictured Mustang is the
custom-colour 'competition
stripe' version, this one in
orange with red stripe.

■ **Fender Bass V 1966**
(main bass, candy apple red) The first five-string bass, the V adds a high C-string to the usual EADG. It has the full 34-inch scale but a short neck, with the fifth string catering for the upper registers. The theory was that it would be easier to play 'across' the strings rather than 'along' the board. Players disagreed, and the V was shortlived.

■ Fender's ads became more colourful during the 60s, reflecting the availability of many models in custom colours. A line-up of the company's 'student' models (above), aimed at beginner players, includes the Mustang Bass (second from left), as well as the unusual electric Mandolin. British Fender ads were more sedate, like this plain example (above left) for the Bass V, from Fender's UK agent of the time, Arbiter.

short 30.5-inch scale with dot-marker rosewood fingerboard, and cherry finish. It was introduced in '61 at $325. As a comparison, Fender's basic list price for the Precision was $229.50 and for the Jazz Bass $279.50.

A number of players were drawn to the throaty EB-3, not least the talented British pair of Jack Bruce (notably in Cream, with big studio bass riffs like 'Politician' or recorded-live workouts such as 'Crossroads') and Andy Fraser (check out his work in Free on the international hit 'All Right Now' or album tracks like 'Mr. Big').

Gibson had launched the single-pickup EB-0 bass in 1959 and modified it to match the new EB-3 look in 1961. A double-neck combining an EB-3 and an SG six-string appeared in 1962, the EBSF-1250. Danelectro had produced probably the first guitar-and-bass double-neck at the end of the 1950s.

In 1963, still with a sharp eye on Fender's growing bass success, Gibson issued a pair of new models, the Thunderbird II and Thunderbird IV. They were the company's first long-scale bass guitars – actually half an inch longer than a Fender – and looked like four-string counterparts to Gibson's Firebird guitar models, also designed by automobile stylist Ray Dietrich. They appeared on Gibson's July 1963 pricelist at $260 for the single-pickup II and $335 for the two-pickup IV. Gibson also pursued Fender by offering the Thunderbirds in a range of custom colour finishes beyond the regular sunburst.

As well as the long scale, Gibson's Thunderbird basses marked a departure for the company with through-neck construction and fully adjustable bridges. Maybe they were too radical, however, because original sales were poor. A revised 'non reverse' Thunderbird design with Gibson's regular glued-in style of neck joint appeared in 1966 after Fender complained about infringements to its patented offset-waist 'reverse' body design.

Over the years, Gibson has remained relatively unsuccessful with bass guitars, although a number of players, mainly from the heavier end of rock, have toyed with the growling Gibson Thunderbird. Most notable was John Entwistle, who started using IVs around 1971 (there's one on *Quadrophenia*), but later Martin Turner (with his melodic lines in Wishbone Ash), Nikki Sixx (Mötley Crüe), and Jared Followill (Kings Of Leon) also strapped on a T'Bird.

To this day, it seems extraordinary that Gibson, one of the world's biggest guitar manufacturers, has never threatened the bass success of its long-standing competitor, Fender. Other than with the Thunderbird, it has never properly adopted the full scale length, and almost always settles for some half-hearted bass version of a regular guitar model. Maybe Gibson just never had staff with enough bass enthusiasm.

What, no frets?

In 1966, Ampeg launched the first fretless bass guitar, the AUB-1. Ampeg was set up in New York in the late 1940s by two double bass players, Everett Hull and Jess Oliver, to market a bass pickup system. In the early 1950s, they began producing bass amplifiers, and from the little Portaflex combo to the industry-standard SVT stack, these are still highly regarded today.

In 1964, Dennis Kager, a guitarist and electronics engineer, had joined the company, by then based in New Jersey. At first his job was to check and adjust the Burns basses and guitars that Ampeg were importing from Britain.

Ampeg had been making an electric mini double bass since 1962, the Baby Bass, a design they'd acquired from the Dopyera Brothers (best known for Dobro resonator guitars) who sold the mini bass under the Zorko brand. Ampeg improved it and Jess Oliver came up with a diaphragm-style pickup, hidden under the pickguard, which the company cleverly called 'the mystery pickup'.

"Bass was the love of the old man," says Kager, referring to Ampeg boss Everett Hull, who was over 60 years old in 1965. "Everything was directed at bass. A lot of the pros playing in New York City would come in, and some would say, 'You guys ought to make a Fender bass.' They would say they'd lost jobs because the studio wanted a Fender bass and they only played double bass."

Ampeg went ahead and started making prototypes of a bass guitar in 1966. They knew how to make necks thanks to the Baby Bass but needed a body. Kager came up with a shape that mixed the offset waist of a Fender Jazz Bass with the rounded base of a P-Bass. But his imagination took a leap when he added two f-holes that went right through the body. "I don't know where that came from," he laughs, "but I thought the top hole could work as a handle to carry the bass."

A 'scrolled' double bass headstock and the diaphragm under-bridge pickup were both borrowed from the Baby Bass. The idea of a fretless fingerboard came from Hull and Oliver. "The double bass players would take the fretted bass guitar, what we called the horizontal bass, and complain that the fingering was different," explains Kager. "The fretless bass guitar was a way of allowing the double bass player to comfortably get into the horizontal bass without so much trouble as the fretted version."[47]

Two models went into production in late 1966, the fretted AEB-1 (Ampeg Electric Bass) and the fretless AUB-1 (Ampeg Unfretted Bass). They sold modestly, remaining as something of a local speciality, and naturally could not compete with Fender's market dominance. Ampeg added further models, again in fretted and fretless versions, including the AMB-1 and AMUB-1 with a

■ A trio of good late-1960s players on this page, starting with **Phil Lesh** (above) of The Grateful Dead, seen here with a modified Gibson EB-3.

■ **Gibson EB-3 1961** (top) Like most Gibsons then, the EB-3 (UK catalogue, above, with EB-0) had a short-scale neck; this and the humbuckers contribute to its deep, muddy tone.

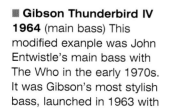

■ **Gibson Thunderbird IV 1964** (main bass) This modified exanple was John Entwistle's main bass with The Who in the early 1970s. It was Gibson's most stylish bass, launched in 1963 with the 'reverse' body and through-neck of the company's Firebird guitars. The two-pickup IV was partnered by a single-pickup II model, featured in the catalogue (opposite).

■ While Gibson fiddled with its bass models, Fender was still attracting many players toward the end of the 1960s and into the 70s. **John Entwistle** (left) used a number of Fender Precisions at that time, including the unusual slab-body version which he's seen tuning here with bandmate Pete Townshend in 1967. **John Paul Jones** (above) moved from a successful studo session career and joined Led Zeppelin in 1968. He relied for a long time in Zep on the 1961 Fender Jazz Bass pictured in this shot from an early gig. He later moved to Alembic basses.

59

conventional magnetic pickup. But as the first commercially available fretless model, the AUB-1 was a significant development. Fender themselves did not offer a fretless bass until the Fretless Precision model of 1970. In more recent years, Bruce Johnson in Burbank, California, began making reissues of the various Ampeg basses.

Plastics and actives

Other guitar companies keen to squeeze more sales from the newly discovered bass guitar market began to experiment and push what they could do with the still relatively young instrument. Ampeg later teamed up with New York guitar repairer Dan Armstrong to produce a distinctive acrylic-bodied 'see-through' bass, as played by Jack Bruce and Bill Wyman.

In Sweden, the Hagstrom company came up with the first eight-string bass guitar, the H-8, in 1967. The idea was to imitate the way strings are laid out on a 12-string guitar, using paired courses of strings and having one string of each pair tuned an octave higher than the regular string. A few contemporary records featured the ringing sound of the H-8, such as Jimi Hendrix's 'Spanish Castle Magic' (recorded October 1967) and Richard Harris's 'MacArthur Park' (1968, played by Joe Osborn).

Some makers' experiments of the late 1960s were geared to expanding the relatively simple electronics used so far in bass guitars. Burns in Britain was the first to incorporate 'active' electronics into a bass: their semi-solid TR-2 model of 1963 featured an on-board battery-powered pre-amplifier so that the player could boost treble and bass tones. Regular 'passive' circuits can only cut from existing tones.

Gibson in the States issued a Les Paul Bass in 1969 (renamed Les Paul Triumph Bass in '71) with low-impedance pickups, designed to offer greater tonal character and quieter operation when connected to low impedance equipment, such as some recording gear. Bass players generally ignored these complicated Gibsons, as well as the company's later Moog-influenced RD basses, which all seemed like they were designed with recording engineers rather than musicians in mind.

Alembicizing the Dead

A more significant development of bass guitar electronics was going on at the same time in an operation about as far removed as possible from the orthodox business environment of a big-league guitar organisation. Alembic started out, as one observer put it, "as more of a concept and a place than a company".[48] The place was San Francisco, the time was 1969, and the motivating force was one Augustus Stanley Owsley.

Owsley's main source of income was from the manufacture of (then legal) LSD, a good deal of which seems to have been consumed by the premier psychedelic group of the time, The Grateful Dead. Part of the community of roadies, friends, and acid freaks that gradually grew up around the Dead was a sort of electronics workshop known as Alembic, named for an apparatus used by distillers (and also apparently by alchemists) "to convey the refined product to a receiver" as the dictionary defines it.

Owsley had created Alembic in the warehouse where The Grateful Dead rehearsed in Novato, California, about 30 miles north of San Francisco. At first the idea was for Alembic to come up with new ways of providing clear, accurate recordings of Dead concerts so that the band could improve their live performances. From this, they became generally interested in improving their studio and live sound quality, mostly by examining and refining all the different elements of the musical process – from instruments and microphones through to the PA systems and recording equipment that came at the end of the chain.

Alembic quickly branched into three main areas, becoming a recording studio, a developer of PA systems, and a workshop for guitar repair and modification. The combination of the woodworking talents of Rick Turner, a one-time Massachusetts folk guitarist and guitar repairer, and the electronics knowledge of Ron Wickersham, who came to Alembic from the Ampex recording equipment company, soon turned the workshop into a proper guitar-making operation.

Alembic became a corporation in 1970 with three equal shareholders: Rick Turner, Ron Wickersham, and recording engineer Bob Matthews.

"We started to customise instruments," explains Turner, "what we called 'Alembicizing'. Some Guild Starfire hollowbody basses were Alembicized for Phil Lesh of the Dead and Jack Casady of Jefferson Airplane in 1970 and 1971." The first official Alembic instrument made to the new company's own design was a bass guitar built for Casady in '71.

By 1973, the Alembic recording studio in San Francisco was becoming a financial headache, but in September of that year a saviour appeared in the shape of a two-page article about Alembic, 'Sound Wizards To The Grateful Dead', in *Rolling Stone* magazine.

Turner says: "The article was seen by the guys at L.D. Heater, which was an instrument distribution company based near Portland, Oregon, owned by Norlin. They had been given a mandate by Norlin to go find some new

Ampeg AEB-1 1966
(main bass) Everett Hull formed the Ampeg company in the late 1940s to make amplifiers and also pickups for double basses. In the early 60s the company produced an electric upright bass, the

Baby model, followed by the first fretless electric bass guitar, the AUB-1 (seen on the wall in the ad, above). The example pictured is the otherwise identical fretted version. The early transducer-style pickup – termed the

'mystery pickup' by Ampeg – is hidden from view under the bridge. The f-holes pass through the body, creating a distinctive and unusual styling. For a number of years the AUB-1 was the only available purpose-built fretless bass guitar.

■ **Raymond 'Boz' Burrell**
(above) pictured on stage
with Bad Company and
playing a fretless Ampeg
bass. Boz also appeared
with King Crimson, earlier in
the 1970s.

■ **Ampeg ASB-1 1967**
(right) This unusual variation
on Ampeg's original bass is
known as the 'devil bass'
thanks to the body horns.
The design was by Ampeg
employee Mike Roman, but
his bizarre body style was
shortlived and only a few
were made. Later in 1967,
Ampeg added a further
variation on the original, the
AMB-1 and AMUB-1, with
regular magnetic pickup.

manufacturers' product to distribute, so they came to us and said, 'What would you do if we gave you a purchase order for 50 instruments?' At that point I think we'd built only 32, but it looked like rescue from bankruptcy to us. So we went to the bank and got enough for me to go and consider how to tool up the Alembic factory."

In that summer '73 *Rolling Stone* feature, Charles Perry described the young Alembic team as "The Grateful Dead family's coven of hi-fi wizards" and quoted them as "aiming for that thing electronic music has, its ability to transcend technology".

Turner was Perry's guide through the Alembic workplaces: he explained to the *Rolling Stone* writer how he had combined his own-design pickups with Wickersham's electronic systems, showed Perry yet another bass being built for the Dead's Phil Lesh, demonstrated the sophisticated controls of a typical Alembic bass, and described the Dead's Alembic PA system.

"All our experimentation is aimed at giving the musician as much control as possible," Turner said. Photos accompanying the piece showed the company's two main premises: the workshop at Cotati, about 40 miles north of San Francisco, where Alembic's woodwork, metalwork, and pickups were made principally by Turner and Frank Fuller, and the Alembic office in nearby Sebastopol where Wickersham dealt with electronics production.

The image projected by the *Rolling Stone* feature was of amiable, talented hippies who rolled with the flow and did their best to indulge the straights of the business world.[49]

"There seemed to be enough cashflow happening by that point, and we had a fairly star-studded clientele, to the point where we got away with it," laughs Turner today in reflective mood. "We started to slowly standardise a regular line of short-scale, medium-scale, and long-scale basses, at first based on the [short-scale humbucker'd] Guild Starfire Bass, and with equivalents in guitars – although at that point we probably made 19 basses or more to every guitar. Bass players were far more interested in a new, clear approach, whereas guitar players seemed satisfied with what they had. Guitar players appear to be inherently more conservative than bass players when it comes to equipment."

Alembic's unique alliance of design elements had been relatively quickly established. The instruments featured a high quality multi-laminate neck-through-body construction, attractive, exotic woods, heavy, tone-enhancing brass hardware, and complex active electronic systems that required external power supplies.

"Heater, our distributor, never knew what we were going to send them; there was no standard wood selection for an Alembic," says Turner. "I'd go buying wood, and what I saw and what I liked I'd get, whether it was California walnut, or myrtle, or zebrawood, padauk, vermilion, cocobolo – whatever. I think Heater turned that to advantage: it was the craftsman's inspiration as to what the woods were going to be, and no two were alike. That became a selling point in itself."[50]

Wickersham describes his experiments with the Alembic bass's active electronics as primarily an attempt to get more high frequencies from the instrument without having to boost the signal at the amplifier. "The pickups in those days had very high inductances," he says, "and we found that even going through a short run of cable reduced a lot of top-end response from them. So we had to mount the active circuit directly into the bass."

Stanley becomes a new bass player

By this time, bassist Stanley Clarke had bought his first Alembic instrument, after Turner had taken an Alembic bass to a Return To Forever gig in San Francisco and invited Clarke, who at the time used a Gibson EB-2, to try it.

Clarke recalls: "He told me in a nice way, 'Look, you really play well, but your sound is atrocious.' So I tried it out and it was great. ... I didn't know what any of it meant, but it sounded the end. And that night on the gig it was like a new bass player had been born. I could suddenly play anything that I heard in my head."[51]

Clarke was born in Philadelphia in 1951 and first played accordion, moving quickly to violin, cello, and double bass and switching to electric bass for high-school bands. His first gigs included work with jazzmen Stan Getz, Dexter Gordon, and Horace Silver.

In the 1970s, Clarke became enormously important, personifying the new breed of bass player and elevating the bass guitar to the role of soloing instrument, an equal partner to the other frontline instruments.

Clarke joined Return To Forever in 1972 alongside the keyboard-playing leader Chick Corea. The group forged a highly successful fusion of jazz, rock, and Latin flavours in the early years of that decade. His first solo album to feature prominent electric bass, titled simply *Stanley Clarke*, appeared in 1974, the beginning of a long line, and these more than any other records established the idea that a virtuoso bass guitarist could become a star.

Ron Wickersham remembers the effect of Clarke using Alembic basses then. "The year the *Rolling Stone* article came out, 1973, was the year that Stanley Clarke bought his instrument, and then people around the world seemed to

Hagstrom H-8 1967
(right) Among the first
production eight-string
basses, the H-8 was built
by the Swedish company
Hagstrom. The strings are
arranged in four pairs, the
second of each pitched an
octave above the regular
string. Use of the big sound
that results is limited to
specialist situations; Jimi
Hendrix featured one on
'Spanish Castle Magic'.

**Gibson Les Paul Bass
1970** Another shortlived
bass, this was quickly
replaced by the Triumph.
Both were based on
existing Les Paul guitars,
underlining Gibson's
tendency to adapt guitar
models into basses.

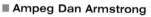

Bill Wyman (below) pictured in the early 1970s playing an Ampeg Dan Armstrong 'see-through' bass, complete with a Rolling Stones tongue logo stuck to the body. Perhaps

Bill and his bandmate Keith Richard, who had the guitar version, followed the handbook instructions and kept the plastic body in good shape by buffing with toothpaste and a soft cloth.

Ampeg Dan Armstrong 1970 (main bass) This was the first solid plexiglas bass, ten years before Steinberger used man-made materials. Dan Armstrong was a guitar repairer from New York City, but his design was shortlived, hindered by conservative players and expensive manufacturing.

learn more about him than of our local San Francisco musicians. So he propelled us. There was a combination of Stanley, whose star was rising very fast promoting us to other high-end musicians, and our new distributor, L.D. Heater, promoting us to the music stores and educating the salesmen in those stores. All of a sudden we were pretty well known pretty fast."[52]

With all of Alembic's deluxe features and monied clients and one-of-a-kind sales talk – even blinking LED lights up the fingerboard if you wanted – the basses were, as you might expect, very expensive. An L.D. Heater brochure from around 1975 shows an Alembic bass pegged at $1,250, at a time when the most expensive new Fender cost $430. Bass players were clearly becoming more willing than guitarists to accept new ideas and designs, and some bassists were beginning to pay for the privilege. Thanks to Alembic, the specialist, high quality, high price bass guitar had arrived.

Neck and neck with graphite

In 1978, Alembic encouraged some experiments with a new material, now generally referred to as graphite. A more accurate term for this composite material made from fibre and resin would be reinforced plastic. Carbon, glass, or graphite fibre, which usually comes as a continuous yarn or 'weave', is saturated with a liquid resin and moulded to produce a thermoset object. The result is not only denser and stiffer than wood but a great deal stronger and much lighter than steel, and it has a greater resistance to extreme temperatures and stress. It was these qualities that attracted Alembic and led them to make some experimental bass necks from graphite.

"We had realised at that point that stiffer was better in a neck," says Rick Turner, "at least in terms of evenness of tone and lack of deadspots." Deadspots are areas on a fingerboard where the note does not ring as clearly or sustain for as long as the other notes. It has proved a notoriously frustrating problem for both maker and player alike.

Geoff Gould was working for an aerospace company in Palo Alto, just south of San Francisco, and was familiar with the graphite material being used for some of the company's satellite parts that required light weight coupled with strength and stability. In 1974, Gould – a bass player – went to a Grateful Dead concert and took a good look at Phil Lesh's 'Alembicized' bass. Assuming it to be a heavy instrument because of all the controls and electronics added on, Gould started to wonder whether a bass made from graphite might be a good idea. He took some graphite samples to Alembic, and they decided to try to make some hollow graphite short-scale bass necks.

At first Gould offered the graphite-neck idea to his aerospace employers as a potential production item. Despite being keen to diversify into consumer products, they declined. Following that, Alembic exhibited a bass with one of the experimental graphite necks at a U.S. instrument trade-show in 1977 and filed a patent just under a year later. Straight after the trade show, John McVie of Fleetwood Mac bought that instrument, the first bass guitar ever to employ graphite technology.

Gould formed Modulus Graphite with other ex-aerospace partners in order to make graphite necks for Alembic, among others, and Modulus produced their own replacement necks and graphite-neck instruments. Turner's name appeared on the graphite-neck patent as inventor, and the patent was assigned to Modulus Graphite.

Turner left Alembic in 1978 and started Turner Guitars (at the time of writing working with Tom Lieber and Stanley Clarke on Spellbinder II basses and making Electroline basses and custom double bass pickups). Modulus also made graphite necks for Music Man for their Cutlass model. Turner sold his share of the patent to Music Man around 1980. The rights to the graphite neck subsequently reverted to Modulus. Gould left the company in 1995 and today makes G. Gould basses and guitars. Meanwhile, Modulus developed the Genesis neck, with wood surrounding a graphite core, and their basses have been notably used by Flea of The Red Hot Chili Peppers. Alembic continues today as a prestigious high-end bass specialist, adding new models to their original Series I and Series II basses over the years.

Graphite was established as a serious new material for bass guitar necks, a low-key rival to wood, and was used intermittently by Alembic and various other makers. Today it also turns up in some bass necks as a strengthening agent in combination with wood.

Spector and a Brooklyn loft

Meanwhile, over in New York, and quite independently, some rather more spectacular applications of graphite were about to take place. This time, the result would be a bass guitar moulded entirely from the material.

Ned Steinberger moved to New York City in the 1970s, after graduating from art school, and started work as a cabinet maker and furniture designer. He soon moved into a space at the Brooklyn Woodworkers Cooperative, which included guitar maker Stuart Spector. Steinberger began to take an interest in Spector's work and discovered that Spector was trying to develop a new bass guitar design.

■ One of the best-known players of Alembic basses was **Jack Casady** (above) of Jefferson Airplane. Casady is pictured here playing Alembic No.001 (see opposite) with Airplane offshoot Hot Tuna.

exotic, active, alembic

■ **Alembic No.001 1971**
(above); **Alembic eight-string 1976** (below)
Alembic's very first bass was made for Jefferson Airplane bassist Jack Casady (who can be seen playing it, with original controls, opposite). It marked the start of a line of instruments that influenced many other bass makers, with exotic woods, active electronics, laminated through-necks, and quality construction. The eight-string pictured here was another custom Alembic, this one made for ELP bassist Greg Lake.

■ **Alembic 'Spider' 1976**
(left) John Entwistle had Alembic make him several of this style of custom bass, heavily influenced by the body shape of Gibson's angular Explorer guitar. This one celebrates Entwistle's classic Who song 'Boris The Spider' by featuring a spider's web made from silver wire inlaid into the body wood. Entwistle had started using Alembic basses a few years earlier and was "blown away" by the sound and playability. He continued to play various Alembic models into the 1980s.

71

Spector first became interested in guitar building when he made an instrument for himself. In the early 1970s, he built guitars and a few SB bass models, which were through-neck basses of conventional shape that sold mainly in the New York area. Spector began to think about a bass design that would have more impact – and by coincidence along came Steinberger.

Steinberger began to suggest ideas and offer help to Spector. Vinnie Fodera, a fledgling bass guitar maker who started working for Spector early in 1977, remembers watching the beginnings of what became a Steinberger–Spector bass guitar design, the NS. Steinberger's first consideration had been the overall construction and ease of production of the proposed bass.

"I developed a system for assembling the body on a neck-blank cut all the way from one end to the other along the line of the outside edge of the fingerboard," says Steinberger. "I combined a nice arch on the top of the instrument, primarily for a visual effect, with another on the back that was primarily for comfort and playability."

The ergonomic Spector–Steinberger bass was launched in 1977 as the Spector NS-1 ('NS' for Ned Steinberger). As the 1980s got underway it influenced a number of other makers (including Warwick, of whom more later), who noticed that the 'curved' body and overall design balanced well and was extremely comfortable to wear and play. Spector later introduced a two-pickup version, the NS-2.

Production of the NS models continued after Spector was bought out by Kramer at the end of 1985. Kramer continued production until early '91, when Kramer folded, and Stuart Spector is now back in business with new models based on the NS design, and since 1998 has traded again as Spector.

Nothing but graphite

Back in the late 1970s, Ned Steinberger had been bitten by the guitar bug and began to formulate ideas for a further bass design. This one had a big impact at the time, almost literally turning many other makers on their heads. One of the things that had troubled Steinberger when he worked on the NS design was the weight of the neck and tuning machines in relation to the body. To counter this, he'd added some weight to the back of the early Spector NS bodies. "And that," says Steinberger, "is what led me to think about taking the tuning machines off the peghead and putting them on to the body."

He wasn't the first to think of this option, but nobody had made anything approaching a commercial impact with such a layout. Steinberger says he made his first headless bass around 1978. It was completely wooden and a disaster –

which led him to consider the opposite of his first attempt: why not make the bass heavier and rigid?

He had already noted deadspots, another drawback of existing bass guitars. While most notes sustain well, certain notes die quickly, primarily because of sympathetic vibrations in a long, thin, wooden neck. So he clamped down his wooden prototype on to a heavy, rigid workbench – and was pleased to get the tone and consistent sustain he was looking for. Steinberger removed the bass from the workbench and sheathed it in stiff fibreglass, a material he'd worked with in furniture-making and boat-building, and found tone and sustain improved. He was on the right track.

"I did other experimentation and realised that the optimum material would be graphite," says Steinberger. "I've always seen graphite as like a superwood." The next move was obvious: to make a proper bass out of graphite. There followed setbacks and trashed trials.

Vinnie Fodera, who was still working with Stuart Spector, recalls Ned conducting many experiments around 1978 in the co-op loft, prior to actually building a bass. Eventually, Steinberger produced his first (probably *the* first) all-graphite bass. Steinberger showed it in public at the 1979 U.S. NAMM trade show in Atlanta, Georgia. It had all the attributes of the final Steinberger Bass: all-graphite construction, tiny rectangular 'body' with tuners on the end, headless neck, and active pickups.

Initially, Steinberger's intention was to sell the design to one of the big guitar companies – he saw himself as a designer, remember, not as a guitar builder – but had zero response. So he decided to make the bass himself and formed the Steinberger Sound Corporation in Brooklyn in December 1980 with three partners: Bob Young (a plastics engineer) and Hap Kuffner and Stan Jay (both of Mandolin Brothers, a Staten Island-based guitar dealer). The new operation launched its Steinberger Bass at the two big musical instrument shows of 1981, at Frankfurt in Germany and Chicago in the States. While many industry people remained sceptical, some musicians warmed to the unusual new bass.

Off with its head!

Ned Steinberger sold his first Steinberger bass, a fretless model, to session bassist Tony Levin, best known then for his work with Paul Simon and King Crimson. "One of the guys who really did us the most good at the start was Andy West of The Dregs," adds Steinberger. "I remember when he played for us at our first music trade show. He stepped up there with his new Steinberger Bass and just played his ass off. I learned a lesson there. We had been getting almost

■ Spector NS-2 1985
(main bass) This first bass
design by Ned Steinberger
appeared in 1977 as the
one-pickup Stuart Spector
NS-1 model. The bass's
comfortable 'curved' body
cross-section (see ad,
opposite) proved popular.

■ Alembic tenor bass 1980 (above) This instrument belongs to **Stanley Clarke**, who used it (and the similar bass he's seen playing opposite) for more than a decade on a variety of solo and collaborative projects. It's the bass upon which

Alembic's later Stanley Clarke Signature series was modelled. Clarke's notable 'lead bass' sound derived from his use of higher-pitched tunings, most often his octave-higher 'piccolo' set-up or the low 'tenor' tone that resulted from the ADGC tuning of this bass.

Spector Guitars Presents The NS-1 Bass Guitar:

A handcrafted limited production instrument with a sculpted contoured body designed to wrap around the musician for maximum comfort.

The instrument features selected hardwoods, rock maple and black walnut or cherry, in the one piece neck body construction. The neck is based on a 36 inch scale which join the body at the 24th fret.

A series I Custom Design DiMarzio pickups, harmonically positioned to enhance punch and clarity, along with a low impedance electronic E. Q. system, greatly expands the tonal variety of the instrument.

The hardware includes gold plated Schaller tuning pegs and a matching Badass bridge. Strap-Lok System's locking strap buttons are also standard equipment.

The NS-1 comes with a hand rubbed finish in either high gloss lacquer or natural penetrating oil and wax.

SPECTOR GUITARS
444 12th Street
Brooklyn, N.Y. 11215
(212) 788-0483

■ Kramer 650B 1977 (this page, centre) Gary Kramer, previously a partner of Travis Bean, set up his own firm to exploit aluminium necks, producing a wide variety of models from 1976 using necks that combined wood and aluminium. But metal still felt odd to some players, and by 1985 the company had rejected aluminium, opting instead for traditional methods. This example is owned by British sessionman Mo Foster.

no interest at the show. And then the night before the last day of the show, Andy got up there and played for the people, and the next day our booth was mobbed. So musicians helped us enormously."

The bass won some prestigious design awards. Magazine reviews praised the strange but effective new instrument. Several other notable and conspicuous players took up the Steinberger Bass, including Sting (Police), Geddy Lee (Rush), and Bill Wyman (Rolling Stones).

Steinberger Sound had a success on their hands. At first they could only make around six basses a month, but by summer 1982 demand exceeded production capacity by 300 per cent, and towards the end of 1983 they were producing as many as 60 instruments a month.

Steinberger: "I think that a key reason why we were able to succeed with this strange headless design made out of plastic was that although at first glance it seemed very strange to a musician, on a second glance it started to make sense, right on the surface. There's a certain logic in the instrument that is visible, that is understandable, that is communicable to bass players. That in my mind is one of the main reasons why we were able to pull off such a radical design."

Like Alembic, Steinberger recognised that bass players then were more interested in new ideas and custom-made instruments than guitarists. "They're not so satisfied with their instruments, which are not so well established, and there's more interest in alternative bass guitars. Also, I think guitar players like to have a lot of different guitars, and don't necessarily want to spend all that much money on them, whereas a bass player is more likely to have just one or two instruments and put everything he's got into those."[53]

The Steinberger headless design was enormously influential in the early 1980s. It seemed almost as if, overnight, guitar-factory workers from New York to Tokyo grabbed their power saws and began creating headless 'designs'. Steinberger was certainly not the first guitar company to have its work copied. Bass designs had long been copied – especially, though hardly exclusively, by oriental companies. But this was almost an epidemic. The new buzzword among electric bass and guitar makers became 'headless'. Active pickups, supplied to Steinberger by California company EMG, also became very widely used on other instruments, and this popularity was another important result of Steinberger's innovations.

Later in the 1980s, in conjunction with Genesis bassist Mike Rutherford and British guitar maker Roger Giffin, Steinberger produced their M series basses and guitars, with a more conventionally styled wooden body bolted to a graphite neck. A variation on the graphite-neck concept with a headless through-neck and wooden body 'wings' had already been popularised in Europe by the British company Status.

In 1986, the Gibson Guitar Corp agreed to buy Steinberger Sound and by 1990 had taken full control of the company. Ned acted as a consultant to Gibson for some time, working on fresh products such as the Steinberger Transtrem transposing vibrato and the DB System detuner bridge. More recently, he has been producing a line of electric small-body string instruments, from double bass to violin, under the NS Design brand. Most are solid wood, although the EU double bass has a body and neck of laminated maple and graphite.

High on piccolo

Carl Thompson was a jazz guitarist who in 1967 began working in Dan Armstrong's guitar repair shop in New York City. When Armstrong closed down some years later, many local players suggested to Thompson that he should open his own shop. He did, and continued to play jazz gigs. On one occasion he was asked to play bass, so he borrowed a Fender. Next day he complained to his partner Joel Frutkin about the shortcomings of the bass guitar. Thompson began, as he puts it, "to think about making a real instrument". The thinking soon translated into action.

He and Frutkin began to build a small number of handmade bass guitars in 1974. New York session players such as Ken Smith became customers. "That same year I was very friendly with Stanley Clarke and Anthony Jackson," says Thompson. "Those guys were hanging out in the shop. They were playing club dates and record dates. I did some fret-jobs on Stanley's [Gibson] EB-2 and on his Alembics when he started playing those. Shortly after, when he first made the big-time, he came in and said he had this idea for making a bass that would be tuned up an octave – and did we think we could do it?"

Despite the fact that Thompson had made only around eight instruments at this point, he persevered with the idea and made the guitar that became known as a piccolo bass. In some ways it wasn't a bass at all. It was tuned E-A-D-G but an octave higher than a bass: almost a regular guitar with two strings missing. However, the first piccolo bass that he made for Clarke had the same 'full' 34-inch scale as a Fender bass. This, and the fact that it was devised by a bass player who played it with a bassist's technique, meant that it was more a high-tuned bass than anything else.

Later, after the 34-inch piccolo bass became damaged, Thompson provided Clarke with a new 32-inch scale piccolo that was Clarke's main high-tuned bass. Clarke has continued to use an array of basses, including standard, tenor (up a fourth to A-D-G-C), and piccolo types, and came to specialise in 'lead bass' playing, even going so far on some performances as to employ an additional bassist to play conventional bass parts below his own soloing.

Clarke first used piccolo bass on his best-selling *School Days* album, recorded in New York City in June 1976, most obviously on the track 'Quiet Afternoon' where he played the main melody on the Carl Thompson 34-inch piccolo bass, overdubbing it above a conventional bass part that he'd played on a regular Alembic four-string. "Stanley put my name on the back of that album and it kind of turned my life around. It made a lot of people aware that there was somebody on the scene called Carl Thompson."[54]

Down with Anthony's contrabass

Within a few weeks of Clarke coming into his shop in 1974 with the piccolo request, Thompson was confronted with another seemingly peculiar idea when session player Anthony Jackson asked if it would be possible to make a six-string bass. Jackson was not thinking of the guitar-down-an-octave style of earlier six-strings, such as the Danelectro UB-2 or Fender VI, which really had been more like baritone guitars than basses.

Jackson proposed to extend the bass guitar's range both upwards and downwards by keeping the standard four strings, tuned E-A-D-G, and adding a high C-string and a low B-string, resulting in a six-string bass tuned B-E-A-D-G-C. The high-C was not in itself a new idea for bass guitar: Fender had used it on the peculiar and shortlived Bass V. But a low B-string was a new concept – and one that would later persuade many bassists to reach for the low notes. In 1974, however, it was simply an unusual idea.

"There were many instances where I just wanted to go lower down," says Jackson about the origins of his low-B idea. "I would detune my Fender bass to get the lower notes when I wanted them, but it was always awkward to do that. It resulted in lower string-tension, which meant I had to raise the bridge and maybe modify the nut. There had to be an easier way to do that. I've always been a fan of pipe organ music – Bach, Messiaen – and I knew I could never hope to get any string as low as the lowest pipes on an organ. However, I felt that I ought to be able to get down another fourth, to B. I knew I was going to call it a contrabass guitar, because the range was below a bass guitar. It was enough to warrant a new name."

He had difficulty finding a maker willing to transform the idea into a guitar. Jackson had not yet climbed to the heights of the session world that he would later reach (he worked with Steely Dan, Paul Simon, and Chaka Khan among many others in the 1980s) and so could not afford to experiment wildly with many expensive custom-made instruments. But Carl Thompson agreed to go ahead and make a stab at the extended six-string bass.

Jackson says he left the details largely to Thompson, who recalls suggesting an extra-long scale-length. But Jackson opted for the 34-inch length he was used to with his Fender. Finding pickups wide enough to extend under all six strings proved almost impossible, but Thompson hired Atilla Zoller, a jazz guitarist with a flair for pickup building, who wound some custom units especially for the six-string. Thompson also had trouble finding a suitable bass string that would accommodate the low-B tuning until D'Addario came up with a specially wound and suitably fat string.

The first extended-range six-string bass guitar finally appeared from Thompson's workshop early in 1975. Jackson was immediately disappointed by the string-spacing, which he had assumed was going to be wider. In the coming decades, five and six-string basses would become more popular and their string-spacing would become wider to suit the finger-style techniques of bassists rather than the plectrum-based styles of guitar players. However, in 1975 this was a brand new field, and no one was sure what to do. Jackson knew that this first attempt at the contrabass guitar wasn't quite right.

He used it on a tour with Roberta Flack, putting down his Fender to play the new six on a couple of songs. "But I didn't have a chance to put it through its paces until I did the first session with it," says Jackson, "which was for the Panamanian saxophone player Carlos Garnett. We did an album called *Let This Melody Ring On* in June 1975, and on one particular tune I used the contrabass. I was absolutely adamant that Carlos should put in the credits 'Anthony Jackson bass guitar and contrabass guitar', which he did. I was very proud of that."[55]

Jackson abandoned the bass after that Flack tour and Garnett recording session – primarily, he recalls, because he found the string-spacing restricting – and returned to his Fender. Jackson and Thompson made some more experimental instruments around 1976, including a fantastic 44-inch-scale trial bass guitar ("unimaginably large and completely unplayable!") and a 36-inch-scale four-string that Jackson did not keep for long. Musician and maker drifted apart, but Jackson continued to dream about the musical usefulness of an extra, low B-string. He was not entirely alone.

Jimmy goes five-string

Jimmy Johnson was working as a freelance bass guitarist in Minneapolis, Minnesota, in the early 1970s, doing jingles and other session work on his low-impedance, phase-switchable, short-scale Gibson Les Paul Bass. "I went to the music store and said it's a shame somebody can't make a long-scale bass with these kind of electronics in it," Johnson recalls. "And they said well, as a matter of fact, there's this company in California called Alembic. So I ordered a four-string Alembic, and this was how I found my way to custom instruments."[56]

Johnson was typical of many players who stumbled on Alembic in the early 1970s and discovered the new idea of the custom-made bass – in other words, a one-off instrument built to your own specifications. Today this has become relatively commonplace – though you still need equally large amounts of cash and bravery – but back then it was a startlingly new concept.

Johnson, probably best known more recently for his fine work with James Taylor, toyed with the idea of an extended bass in the mid 1970s. With such a bass, he would be able to play notes below the conventional low E-string. Like quite a few players, he occasionally detuned his four-string as a means of venturing into lower-pitched playing. His father, who played double bass in a Minnesota orchestra, had an instrument fitted with a mechanical 'machine'. This relatively common option for orchestral basses consists of a headstock-mounted fingerboard extension allowing the player to switch an extra-long E-string down as low as C.

At first, Johnson and his father tried to figure a way of building a similar extension onto an electric bass guitar. They soon decided against this – but it's interesting to note that, once again, someone somewhere else was thinking independently along similar lines. The Kubicki company, founded by Philip Kubicki in California, would launch its Ex-Factor electric bass guitar in the early 1980s with exactly this kind of headstock extension, allowing the lower end of the E-string to go down by an extra two frets.

Kubicki's stylish and ergonomically pleasing bass was described in the company's advertising as "the world's first electric extended bass". Stu Hamm used it to incorporate the independently co-ordinated two-hand tapping style that appeared during the late 1980s. Later, the retrofitting Hipshot D-Tuner provided a similar facility for other basses and has since become an important tool for many players.

Meanwhile, back in the mid 1970s, Jimmy Johnson and his father were dissuaded from a similar 'extension', primarily by the comments of string manufacturer GHS, who said it would be more difficult to make a long string than it would be to make a standard-length string with a wide diameter. Johnson was aware, again from his father's orchestral background, that some players used five-string double basses with an extra low-B string.

In 1975, Johnson ordered a custom five-string bass from Alembic. He knew that they already offered such a model, which they expected to supply with an additional high-C string, presumably for those who wanted to play occasional higher-pitched 'lead bass' parts, probably influenced by Stanley Clarke and his piccolo bass.

Johnson ordered an Alembic five-string and it arrived in 1976. He modified the nut and bridge to take his special GHS low-B string, and found himself with a B-E-A-D-G tuning. It was probably the first ever low-B five-string bass guitar. With increasingly wider string-spacing, the low-B five-string bass would become an important addition to the bass player's kit during the coming decades and is today an essential item for many players.

Longing for six

Back on the east coast, Anthony Jackson found a new bass-maker who agreed to build him another six-string 'contrabass' guitar. Ken Smith was a New Yorker who collected and dealt in double basses and worked as a session man, playing double bass and bass guitar on what he describes as everything from Shirley Bassey and Broadway musicals to jingles and commercials.

In the mid 1970s, Smith wondered why bass guitars couldn't be made to sound as pure and free of deadspots as the best double basses. He discussed these ideas with maker Carl Thompson and as a result bought Thompson's third custom-made instrument. But still Smith thought he could do better and resolved to start making bass guitars in his own right.

In late '79, Smith had Thompson make up a rough 'carcass' bass from a design he'd sketched out. He took this bare-bones bass to Stuart Spector's workshop at the co-op loft in Brooklyn and contracted Spector and co-worker Vinnie Fodera to produce the original Ken Smith basses. Fodera says that the first 32 Smith basses were made at Spector and that he did most of the work; Spector says they produced the finished woodwork and Smith assembled them. Anthony Jackson bought one of these four-string basses and, meanwhile, convinced Smith that he should make a six-string contrabass guitar.

Smith decided to set up his own workshop in summer 1980 and, logically, asked Fodera to run the new shop. Fodera agreed, left Spector, had the Ken Smith workshop up and running by early 1981, and started work with a revised body shape for the new Ken Smith BT bass guitars (BT stood for the onboard 'Bass and Treble' active circuit).

Fodera specifies the importance of Ken Smith in the bass world of the early 1980s. "He might have been the first guy to give basses a kind of connoisseur

■ Steinberger prototype 1979 (below) The first bass design by Ned Steinberger had resulted in the Spector NS models, but his next idea was much more dramatic. This is the third of three prototypes, good enough to be shown at a '79 instrument fair.

■ Status Series II 1989 (below) British maker Rob Green helped popularise the headless idea and the graphite through-neck style with body 'wings'. The more familiar styling attracted a number of players, especially in Europe.

■ **Steinberger L-2 1980**
(main bass) One of the first
production models of the
startling Steinberger bass,
the L-2 was the two-active-
pickups version, alongside
the one-active L-1 and the
passive-pickup H-1 and H-2
models. Steinberger's
radical design combined
plastic materials, a very
different new shape, and
those active pickups. A
regular headstock was
discarded, with tuners
added to the body, which
was trimmed down to a
minimal size.

■ Steinberger's striking new
look, as well as his new
ideas about what a bass
could be, soon had some
key players lining up to play
the instruments that the
Brooklyn-based company
produced. One of the first
was sold to Tony Levin (Paul
Simon, King Crimson), with
other notable Steinberger
men including Sting (Police),
Geddy Lee (Rush; pictured
right in 1983), and Bill
Wyman (Rolling Stones). In
1986, Gibson bought
Steinberger and by 1990
had taken full control. Ned
Steinberger acted as a
consultant before setting up
his own NS Design brand in
recent years.

attitude. He was a skilled musician designing and building his very own high-quality original instruments, different from whatever else was on the market at the time and bearing his own name. It was the first designer bass, if you will, at a very high price, and very exotic in every detail. He carried it further."[57]

Jackson was convinced that he needed wide string-spacing on a six-string bass. But Smith was not so sure, and the first Ken Smith six-string bass, built for Jackson at the end of 1981 by Fodera at the Smith shop, still had relatively narrow string-spacing.

"It was much better than Carl's but the string spacing was too narrow," Jackson recalls of that bass. Nonetheless, he managed to tour widely and record some 50 albums using it, and the bass became something of a research testbed, with pickups and electric circuits regularly changed. The bass was Jackson's sole tool from summer 1982, when he decided to leave the Fender at home and use the Smith six-string exclusively, including on the sessions for Paul Simon's *Hearts And Bones* album.

Grooving with a low B

Anthony Jackson's second Ken Smith six-string came along in 1984, still with a 34-inch scale but revised in terms of weight and feel – and with a small plate that noted it as a Smith–Fodera. In order to have spacing between the strings similar to that of Jackson's Fender four-string but across all six strings, the bass was fitted with an extra-wide neck and fingerboard. While this massive width looked decidedly odd, the bass was significant as the first extended-range six-string bass guitar with wide string-spacing.

"I was very highly criticised by other instrument builders," says Ken Smith of the wide-spaced six, "by weight and by how wide this is – they said it looks like a battleship. But then a couple of years later they're all trying to chop into my business, only they're making 100 a week and I'm making two a week."[58]

Its owner was very happy with his new contrabass guitar. "It was," concludes Jackson, "the first really viable instrument. I had realised the problem was in the wood and in the basic design of the first one, which was massive and heavy, and at the time everybody thought that was essential for sustain. I made a lot of recordings with this 1984 six-string, too, and it had the least deadspots of any instrument I'd ever played. It was a milestone."[59]

Fodera had parted from Smith in 1983, acquiring the existing workshop and continuing to work from there, setting up Fodera Guitars with partner Joey Lauricella. But they carried on building Ken Smith basses under contract until 1985 and also began making their own Fodera bass guitars, including a low-B five-string model and, from 1986, six-string contrabass guitars for Jackson. At the time of writing, Fodera is still in Brooklyn and continues to make the six-string model, known as the Anthony Jackson Presentation Contrabass Guitar, alongside signature basses for Victor Wooten and Matthew Garrison, as well as various other models. Ken Smith too continues to build good basses and is now based in Perkasie, Pennsylvania.

The biggest change for the new Fodera six-strings in the 1980s was a move to an extra-long 36-inch scale, which improved the tone and tension of the low-B in particular.

Around the middle of the decade, Fodera was not alone in using an extra-long scale to enable low tuning: Modulus in America used a 35-inch scale on their basses while Overwater in England used a 36-inch scale for their C-Bass, a four-string tuned down two full steps to C-F-Bb-Eb.

The 1985 C-Bass was designed in conjunction with ex-Graham Parker & The Rumour bassist Andrew Bodnar, who was looking for a stage bass on which he could reproduce low-pitched basslines originated in the studio on synthesisers, without consideration of the standard bass guitar's threshold of low-E.

Jackson blazed a trail for the six-string bass from those pioneering years of the first Carl Thompson experiments of the mid 1970s. (Thompson continues to make custom basses today; his customers include Les Claypool of Primus.)

But of greatest significance for the general development of the bass guitar was the extra low string, employed and popularised during subsequent decades in the shape of the wide-spaced five-string bass guitar, tuned B-E-A-D-G.

While the six-string bass has been put to use by a relatively small number of players, mainly in jazz and fusion, the five-string has become an essential tool for many touring and recording bassists in all styles of music. Today, a five-string model appears on most good bass-maker's pricelists. Fender, for example, added a five-string Jazz Bass in 1990 and a Precision in '99. The low-B five is here to stay.

From funk to punk

Among the players who stretched the musical horizons of bass guitar in the 1970s were a pair of funk pioneers, Bootsy Collins and Bernard Edwards. They helped to define funk bass at each end of the decade.

Bootsy found himself in James Brown's band after the boss fired the previous outfit – following 'demands' – and hired Bootsy's mob. Bootsy did an appropriately funky job in Brown's band, including the recording of the impossibly convoluted bassline on 'Sex Machine' in 1970, and then went on to

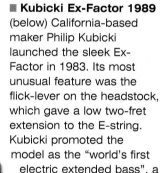

■ **Kubicki Ex-Factor 1989**
(below) California-based maker Philip Kubicki launched the sleek Ex-Factor in 1983. Its most unusual feature was the flick-lever on the headstock, which gave a low two-fret extension to the E-string. Kubicki promoted the model as the "world's first electric extended bass", a reference to the fact that some double basses had long been offered with a similar 'extension' feature.

carl thompson basses

"The Stradivari of the Electric Bass. . . and he makes a helluva chicken sandwich."
-Les Claypool

Each instrument is completely <u>hand carved</u>
by Ron Blake and Carl Thompson. **Serious inquiries call (718)852-1771**

■ **Fodera Jackson Contrabass 1989** (main bass, top) The origins of the modern low-B five-string and six-string basses are complex and are explained in detail in the text. Some of the key players in the development were session bassist **Anthony Jackson** (owner of this Fodera, which he is seen playing on-stage at a Paul Simon concert, above), maker Carl Thompson (whose custom fretless six-string is seen with **Les Claypool** of Primus, above left), and makers Ken Smith and Vinnie Fodera.

create some startling low-note magic in George Clinton's P-Funk projects, Parliament and Funkadelic, not least on Parliament's 1975 classic *Mothership Connection*. On stage, Bootsy often played a strange star-shaped custom bass made by Larry Pletz (and later replicated by Washburn).

Meanwhile, Bernard Edwards provided the solid, rolling grooves underneath the smooth disco-funk of Chic (check out the remarkable 'Good Times' from 1979), primarily on Music Man and B.C. Rich basses. Edwards contributed further classic lines to Chic's outside production projects made in collaboration with his guitarist partner Nile Rodgers, including the relentless 'We Are Family' by Sister Sledge.

More rock-hard 1970s grooves came from players such as Paul Jackson on Herbie Hancock's mesmeric *Head Hunters* album (1973), Rocco Prestia with the mighty funk machine of Tower Of Power (take a listen to 'You Got To Funkifize' on 1972's *Bump City* or 'What Is Hip' on the following year's *Tower Of Power*), George Porter's rich, chunky lines with The Meters (treat yourself to a compilation like *Funkify Your Life*), and Nathan Watts's wonderful Stevie Wonder work (check out 'Sir Duke' and 'I Wish' from 1976's *Songs In The Key Of Life*).

Meanwhile, Chris Squire played with British progressive rock band Yes, and his surging, contrapuntal lines did much for the rebirth of interest in Rickenbacker basses during the early 1970s. 'Roundabout' on *Fragile* (1972) is a good place to start if you've never experienced Squire's impressive style and the ultra-bright tone he draws from his Rick 4001S.

Punk, pop, new wave, and metal all made a mark in the decade too: try Jean-Jacques Burnel picking his prominent P-Bass throughout The Stranglers' hits, the brilliant Rutger Gunnarsson throughout Abba's sophisticated productions, Dave Allen powering away underneath The Gang Of Four, or metal guru Roger Glover at the bottom of Deep Purple's upended heavy riffing.

And let's not forget the magical Chuck Rainey, a busy sessionman since the mid 1960s but heard to superb effect on stylish Steely Dan cuts such as 'Kid Charlemagne' (*The Royal Scam*, 1976) and 'Peg' (*Aja*, 1977).

In reggae, it's as much the spaces that count, with few bassists more adept than Aston 'Family Man' Barrett in Bob Marley's band (hear the key '70s trio of albums *Burnin'*, *Natty Dread*, and *Live!*).

Another towering talent is Robbie Shakespeare, always right down there among the low notes and often in tandem with drummer Sly Dunbar, on albums that include classics by Burning Spear (*Marcus Garvey*, 1975) and Peter Tosh (*Legalize It*, 1976).

Slap that bass

Slapping was a technique that some double bass players had used for decades. They would literally slap the strings with their picking hand in order to get more volume from their acoustic instruments.

As the great Hollywood-musical lyricist Ira Gershwin put it in 1937: "Slap that bass, slap it till it's dizzy, slap that bass, keep the rhythm busy." Rockabillys, too, took up the idea with great gusto in the 1950s (and in subsequent revivals).

The first time that many bass guitarists noticed a musician applying a modern version of the idea to the electric bass was when Larry Graham came to prominence around 1970 in Sly & The Family Stone (and not too long afterwards in his own group, Graham Central Station). Graham used his 1960 Jazz Bass to popularise the slap style. With his right-hand, he would bounce the edge of his thumb off one of the lower strings while also pulling higher strings, in various rhythmic combinations, generating a powerfully percussive sound.

'Everyday People' on Sly's *Stand* (1969) is a good example of early slap – and there's a satisfying bass-manifesto moment on 1968's 'Dance To The Music' when Larry sings right down low: "I'm gonna add some bottom, so the dancers just can't hide." But it would be an oversight not to direct your ears to Larry's remarkable 'Hair' on *Graham Central Station* (1973) or 'Jam' from the same band's *Ain't No 'Bout-A-Doubt It* (1975).

With its roots in early-1970s funk, bass-guitar slap crossed over into jazz and fusion and really took hold in the 1980s, when it infiltrated all manner of musical styles. The technique became required knowledge among bassists, even generating instructional books and videos dedicated entirely to its practice. More recently, the slapping has subsided.

Stand by for StingRay

The active electronics systems popularised in the early 1970s by Alembic began to find their way into less expensive instruments produced by other companies, and few with more success than Music Man. Leo Fender and ex-Fender employees Forrest White and Tom Walker set up the firm in 1972, originally as Tri-Sonics, then as Musitek, and finally, in 1974, as Music Man.

When CBS had purchased the Fender companies, the corporation gave Leo a contract with a ten-year non-competition clause that expired in 1975. In April of that year, Leo Fender was announced as president of Music Man Inc.

The first Music Man bass was the single-pickup StingRay with active electronics. The bass was easily identified visually by its distinctive three-and-one tuner layout at the headstock. Production of the StingRay started in June

■ Modulus Graphite Quantum six-string 1984 (main bass) Modulus was originally set up to develop the new idea of carbon graphite necks, which the company produced for Alembic, Music Man, and Zon. The bass shown here has an extra-long 35-inch scale to help the fidelity of the low B-string, and features a tighter string-spacing than most modern sixes. Note how the strings mount directly into the body, underlining the strength of graphite.

■ **Ken Smith BT Custom VI 1993** (opposite) Smith was an ex-professional bassist turned bass maker and was among the pioneers of the modern multi-string bass with wide string-spacing and low-B tuning. Smith continues to make instruments today.

■ A quartet of influential bassists from the 1970s: **Chris Squire** (opposite) added classy bass to Yes; **Bootsy Collins** (top left) was a brilliant funk showman; metal guru **Roger Glover** (top) gave Deep Purple a foundation; and **Aston Barrett** (above) created reggae space in Bob Marley's Wailers.

1976 and it was an almost instant hit, remaining popular to this day and considered by many players as Leo's successful active update of his Fender Precision Bass design.

Music Man instruments were at first manufactured by Leo's CLF Research company in Fullerton. But after Music Man tried unsuccessfully to buy CLF in 1978, Leo decided to break away and set up his own new operation, G&L, the following year. Leo's associate Dale Hyatt recalled Leo saying he had nothing to do with Music Man after 1978, when he pulled out of the business. G&L started production by 1980, and the new company's output too featured some good basses, including the two-pickup active L-2000 model.

Music Man continued to make instruments in Fullerton for a while but was eventually folded and sold to string-maker Ernie Ball in March 1984. The following year, the new owners moved the operation north, near to their existing string and accessory works in San Luis Obispo, where Music Man basses and guitars remain successfully in production today. The StingRay 5 five-string model joined the line in 1988.

Early players of the Music Man StingRay in the 1970s underlined its versatility: Carl Radle often used one in Eric Clapton's band during the decade to lay down his effortless rock grooves, while Louis Johnson of The Brothers Johnson proved the Music Man's worth in funk, popularising its suitability for the slap style. Johnson exploited the StringRay's on-board battery-powered active electronics that enabled the bass and treble tones to be boosted, resulting in a sound with much reduced middle frequencies when compared to the passive Precision Bass. It also became clear to many players that a hard maple fingerboard seemed to assist the sound of slap.

In 1983, Pino Palladino's lyrical fretless StingRay pricked up listeners' ears when he featured it prominently on the introduction to Paul Young's hit version of Marvin Gaye's 'Wherever I Lay My Hat (That's My Home)'. Palladino has since had a successful session career, with everyone from Simon & Garfunkel to The Who, D'Angelo to John Mayer, and now often plays a Fender Precision.

Fender in the seventies

At Fender, a sense of history was dawning. In 1971, a CBS Musical Instruments ad noted the 20th anniversary of Fender's introduction of the bass guitar. "The Precision Bass is the granddaddy of all electric basses," ran the blurb. "It was the first one on the market and almost 20 years later is still the standard of the music industry."[60] There was no arguing with that: Fender basses were everywhere. Some Fenders of the period were fitted with a 'bullet' truss-rod adjuster: it appeared on the revised 1972 Telecaster Bass and from about 1975 on the Jazz Bass. ('Bullet' described the appearance of the truss-rod adjustment nut at the headstock.)

Early in 1972, Fender announced new natural finishes for most major models, including Precision and Jazz, on solid ash bodies. This together with the often-seen maple fingerboard option (and black block markers on the Jazz) set the look that many players associate with 1970s Fenders.

During this decade and into the next, a common retrofit by some bassists to their Fenders was the Badass bridge, a more substantial update of Leo's original that is still popular today. There was a general trend at this time for replacing other bits and pieces of bass hardware, made by companies such as Schechter, DiMarzio, and Mighty Mite.

Fenders from the early 1970s came with the company's new high-gloss 'thick skin' finish, achieved by spraying more than a dozen coats of polyester on to the unfortunate instrument, and today dismissed by some for its plastic appearance and giveaway period vibe. Fender's press release enthusiastically described the new finish as "bringing out the natural beauty of the wood beneath a tough protective coating".

Marketing director Dave Gupton announced that 1972 was a record year for Fender, with unit production and dollar sales figures both higher than ever before. He was in little doubt that 1973 would yield still higher figures and that the trend would continue upward. A major expansion programme was on at the Fullerton plant to boost output still further. Completed in summer 1974, it provided a new total of 289,600 square feet of production, warehouse, and shipping space. A few years later, Fender proudly announced it employed 750 workers there.

All this allowed CBS to manufacture in much greater numbers. They were selling 40,000 Fender instruments a year by the end of the 1970s. A further sign of this vastly increased production was the end of the tradition for putting a date on an instrument's neck. Since the earliest days of the first Fender models, workers had almost always pencilled and later rubber-stamped dates on the body-end of necks. It remains about the most reliable way to date a Fender (leaving aside the question of fakes). But from 1973 to the early 1980s, Fender stopped doing it. Presumably they were simply too busy.

Fretless pioneers

The name of Jaco Pastorius has become almost synonymous with the fretless bass guitar, for it was in his hands during the late 1970s that the instrument

■ **Music Man StingRay Bass 1976** (main bass) Music Man basses became Leo's second success story, with the StingRay in particular building on his already sizeable reputation for the classic Fender Precision and Jazz models.

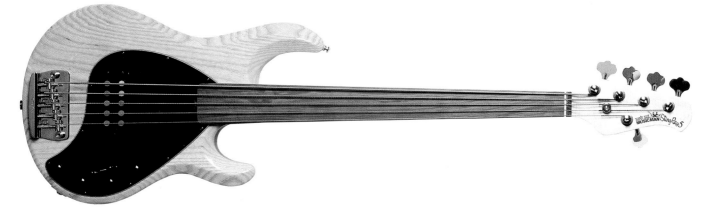

■ **Music Man StingRay 5 Bass fretless 1989**
(above) Music Man was started by ex-Fender men Forrest White and Tom Walker in 1970, joined in '75 by Leo Fender, who added basses and guitars to the existing amps. His StingRay was an attempt to improve on earlier work, featuring a new headstock layout and effective active electronics. Leo broke away from Music Man to set up his own G&L firm (ad, left) in 1979. Music Man was bought by Ernie Ball in 1984.

■ Slapping became a popular technique in the 1980s. It was popularised by **Larry Graham** (opposite, top left) in Sly & The Family Stone and Graham Central Station, and **Louis Johnson** (right, with Music Man).

came alive for the first time. But Pastorius was by no means the first player to use fretless bass; his achievement, as we'll see, was to popularise its sound by bringing it right up front, playing it in a virtuosic manner as a featured instrument.

The fretless bass, with its smooth, unfretted fingerboard, enables bassists to achieve a sound completely different to that of the fretted instrument. Notes swell with a beautifully warm tone and the fretless player can easily execute an impressive slide – sometimes called a 'gliss', an abbreviation of glissando – or incorporate longitudinal string vibrato. To get similar sounds, some players had tried electric upright basses of the early 1960s, such as the double-bass-shaped Ampeg Baby Bass or the skeletal German-built Framus Triumph Bass, nicknamed the 'pogo stick'. Neither proved very successful, although in more recent years there has been a significant revival of electric uprights.

Bill Wyman came up with a very early fretless bass guitar in 1961 when he decided to modify a cheap Dallas Tuxedo fretted bass. He says: "With the help of a neighbour's fretwork machine, I reshaped the guitar body and then took all the frets out. I intended replacing them with new ones, but it sounded so good that I left it as it was – the first fretless bass."

He soon bought a Framus fretted bass, but says he continued to play the home-made bass in the studio for many years "as it gave me the perfect sound".[61] Even if Wyman's contributions to Rolling Stones records don't remind us today of the modern fretless sound, his home-made bass seems at least to have prompted him to some adventurous slides – as heard on cuts like '19th Nervous Breakdown', 'Paint It Black', and 'Mother's Little Helper' (all 1966) and 'We Love You' ('67). He can be seen recording with the fretless on 'Sympathy For The Devil' in the 1968 Jean-Luc Godard film *One Plus One*.

After that peculiarity, among the earliest well-known players of fretless bass guitar was Rick Danko of Americana pioneers The Band. Danko was primarily a fretted-Fender player, but Ampeg gave him a number of instruments around 1970, including an AMUB-1 fretless. Danko quickly modified the Ampeg with Fender pickups.

"I used the Ampeg on about 80 per cent of our *Cahoots* album of 1971," recalled Danko, who also used it for the late-1971 concert that became the *Rock Of Ages* live album. "It's a challenge to play fretless," he said, "because you have to really use your ear."[62]

A striking, influential appearance of the instrument in pop music came with Bad Company's summer 1974 hit single 'Can't Get Enough' that had Boz Burrell's fretless Precision well to the fore. Kenny Passarelli had given a fretless P-Bass an earlier outing on Joe Walsh's 1973 album *The Smoker You Drink, The*

Player You Get, notably on 'Days Gone By', while Sting popularised the idea later in the decade when he played various fretless basses live with The Police.

Another early exponent of the fretless was Ralphe Armstrong, who used a hybrid Fender with Jazz body and fretless Precision neck during his tenure with John McLaughlin's jazz-rock band Mahavishnu Orchestra – recording *Apocalypse* (1974) and *Visions Of The Emerald Beyond* (1975) – and later with electric violinist Jean-Luc Ponty.

Portrait of Jaco

John Francis Pastorius III was born in Norristown on the outskirts of Philadelphia, Pennsylvania, in 1951 and moved with his family to Fort Lauderdale, Florida, eight years later. His father was a professional drummer. Jaco took up the drums too, joining a teenage jazz band at age 13 and moving to bass guitar in 1967. He went on to a variety of pro work: everything from touring with R&B bands to playing cruise-ship easy listening.

In 1975, Jaco's dues paid off and he took a giant step, recording with Pat Metheny on the jazz guitarist's *Bright Size Life* album, notably on 'Round Trip/Broadway Blues'. The following year, Jaco joined the jazz-rock group Weather Report, with whom he stayed for six eventful years.

The band had been formed in '71 by keyboardist Joe Zawinul and saxophonist Wayne Shorter. Both had been members of the experimental jazz-rock line-ups of Miles Davis's band in the late 1960s. They acquired a taste there for fusing rock's amplified rhythms with the moody freedom of modal jazz, a combination they developed in Weather Report.

Jaco's pioneering use of the fretless bass guitar with its singing, sustained quality and his tremendous harmonic and melodic skills on the instrument coincided with some of Weather Report's finest recorded compositions and daringly improvisational live work, nearly always with his bass prominently positioned in the mix.

Weather Report became one of the most commercially successful jazz-rock bands. Their best known piece from the period is 'Birdland' from *Heavy Weather* (1977), an intricate weave of sounds and textures enlivened by Jaco's strong bass work. Jaco's showcase 'Teentown' on the same album is jaw-dropping stuff.

Most bass players had their earliest encounter with the sounds of Jaco's playing when they heard his first solo album, *Jaco Pastorius*, released in 1976. (Weather Report's *Black Market* came out about the same time, with Jaco on just two tracks.) He had two Fender Jazz Basses that stayed with him for most

■ A trend began during the 1970s for upgrading and – the hope was – improving an existing bass by replacing pieces of the hardware. Something that players would have done in their own way was turned into a mini-industry. The fad for 'hot' replacement pickups saw DiMarzio leading the pack: this ad from 1980 (above, left) shows some split pickups on a B.C. Rich bass. A common retrofit to Fenders was the Badass bridge (1978 ad, above centre), a substantial update of Leo's original that still appears today. Fender had some druggy ads in the 1970s, with Alice In Wonderland inspiring this one (above, right). "Of course," said Alice, "nine out of ten pick on a Fender bass."

■ **Fender Telecaster Bass 1972** (above); **Fender Jazz Bass 1977** (below) The Telecaster Bass had been Fender's first attempt at a reissue, but in this second version the original single-coil was swapped for a humbucker, flavour of the decade. Maple necks were very 1970s too, and the Jazz Bass of the period had pearloid position markers. It also had a 'bullet' truss-rod adjuster at the headstock.

■ **Fender Precision Bass 1979** (main bass) The Precision marched on as one half of Fender's still dominant bass duo. Fender's 1977 ad (right) stressed versatility. By now, the maple neck was a familiar look, as was the black laminated pickguard. But the 80s would prove a confusing decade for Jazz and Precision, with many variations on the theme.

of his career: a fretted 1960 model and a de-fretted 1962. He played the fretless '62 on most of the tracks on that solo album, including the captivating double-tracked 'Continuum' that defined the Jaco fretless sound.

The fretted Jazz appeared on just two tracks, 'Come On Come Over' and the much-imitated 'Portrait Of Tracy', which demonstrated Jaco's remarkable use of harmonics. (Natural harmonics, to give them their full name, are ringing high-pitched notes that the bassist produces by touching rather than fretting strategic points on the strings.)

Pastorius said that he'd been using both his Jazz Basses since about 1971. As he paid only $90 for the secondhand fretless Jazz it seems unlikely that he could have afforded a new bass – but anyway, there wouldn't have been many new fretless basses for him to buy in 1971.

About all that was available in America were three recently launched models: a Hohner, an Ovation, and Fender's Precision Fretless, issued around 1970. The Hohner and Ovation made little impression, and the Fender was poorly received: double bass players felt the sound was too muffled and ill-defined, while bass guitarists found the instruments hard to pitch accurately.

Some players keen to achieve a fretless sound had no choice but to unlock their toolkits and take matters into their own hands. Pastorius said that someone had already removed the frets from the '62 Jazz when he bought it. "Looked like somebody had taken a hatchet to it, so I had to fix it up," he laughed. Jaco painted glossy epoxy over the de-fretted fingerboard to give it a smooth feel. "I've always been playing fretless bass, and I've had a few other fretless basses that I had to take the frets out of myself," he said.

Pastorius complained that the sliding, growling bass sounds on his 1976 solo album had meant that some listeners – few of whom had probably heard a fretless bass or even knew that such a thing existed – had assumed that he must have been playing double bass. He had tried double bass without success, he explained. "It's a pain in the ass. It's just too much work for too little sound. I love to play with drummers, and it's next to impossible to play upright bass with a drummer. No matter how loud you get you're not loud enough."[63]

Despite Jaco's post-Weather Report band Word Of Mouth, and his career-high contributions to Joni Mitchell's *Hejira* (1976), *Mingus* (1979), and the live *Shadows And Light* (1980), his life was cut tragically short. Amid drug-related problems, he died in a bar brawl in September 1987 at the age of just 35.

Joni Mitchell said: "The day after Jaco died, I went back and listened to *Mingus*. I went back, basically, to reminisce. And gee, there was some beautiful communication in that playing. I hadn't listened to it for years. The grace of the improvisation on that record ... I thought that was some really good playing. And there were a lot of magic evenings like that."[64]

Strangely, Fender did nothing to capitalise on the success and popularity of Pastorius for some time and rather surprisingly did not produce a fretless option for a Jazz Bass until the mid 1980s; such apparently obvious marketing was left largely to oriental makers and custom builders. A Fender Jaco Pastorius Jazz Bass Fretless appeared in 1999 – even then commissioned by the Bass Centre of Los Angeles – and a Custom Shop Jaco Pastorius Tribute Jazz Bass came along three years later.

Any number of bassists could be heard from the late 1970s onward "doing a Jaco" by playing prominent, melodic fretless basslines – whether on production fretless instruments or do-it-yourself de-fretted basses. Some brave bass players preferred a fretless with a plain, unmarked fingerboard, while others opted for the reassurance of inlaid lines where the frets would have been, the 'lined fretless' as it became known. But it was Jaco who opened many players' ears to a new world of possibilities from the fretless bass guitar, and he remains one of the most influential and revered bassists of all time.

Fender copies Fender

At the beginning of the 1980s, Japanese-made bass guitars were growing in importance and becoming more accepted. The Japanese had started emulating classic American instruments in the early 1970s, and most Western makers didn't see much to worry about.

Later, the quality of the oriental instruments improved, but some American makers still kept their heads stuck firmly in the sand. Dave Gupton, vice president of Fender in 1978, said: "Fender is not adversely affected by the Japanese copies as perhaps some of the other major manufacturers, because we have been able to keep our costs pretty much in line."[65]

That casual attitude changed dramatically in a few short years. By the dawn of the 1980s, the dollar had soared in value relative to the yen. Coupled with the high quality of many Japanese basses, this meant that instruments built in the orient were making an impact on the market. Several Japanese companies made significant leaps in design and construction and had taken on board some of the ideas of high-end U.S. producers, including specific features such as the active electronics and visible through-neck of Alembic as well as more general trends such as the low-B five-string.

Brands that incorporated these features and benefits into their relatively affordable instruments included Ibanez (with the Musician series, as used by

■ Fender Precision Bass fretless 1973 (below) Fretless basses had begun with Ampeg's innovations in the mid 1960s. The instrument's smooth, unfretted fingerboard was a mini version of that on a double bass, and enabled electric bassists to achieve a very different sound to that of the conventional fretted instrument. Notes can be made to 'swell' with a beautifully warm tone, and of course the fretless player can more easily execute slides. Fender finally offered a fretless version of the Precison Bass in 1970, like the one shown here, at the same price ($293.50) as the regular fretted version.

■ Fender Jaco Pastorius Tribute Jazz Bass 1999 (main bass) Jaco Pastorius released his first solo album (jacket below) in 1976, the same year he joined Weather Report. Bass players were intrigued by Jaco's remarkable skills, deployed on a pair of Jazz Basses, one fretless, like the Tribute replica pictured here, the other fretted (seen with Jaco on stage, below). He popularised the sound of fretless bass, with Weather Report and through his peerless contributions to a series of Joni Mitchell albums in the late 1970s.

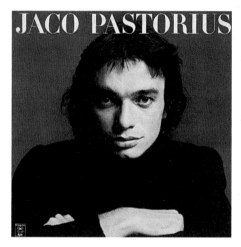

Sting), Aria (used by several British bassists, including John Taylor of Duran Duran), and Yamaha (whose BB-5000 narrow-spaced five-string was a strong seller in America thanks to the influence of players such as Nathan East).

Over at Fender at the start of the 1980s, CBS wanted some new blood to reverse failing fortunes. They recruited three key men from the American arm of Yamaha: John McLaren became head of CBS Musical Instruments overall; Bill Schultz was Fender president; and Dan Smith became director of marketing electric guitars. They discovered that Fender barely knew how to properly make their key quartet of Precision, Jazz, Strat, and Telecaster any more. Schultz recommended a big investment package to modernise the factory – which effectively stopped U.S. production while the changes were made.

Another recommendation was to start alternative production of Fenders in Japan. Fender's sales were being hammered by oriental copyists, who made their biggest profits at home in Japan. Fender would hit back at them in Japan by making and selling guitars there.

A joint venture was established in 1982 combining the forces of Fender and two Japanese distributors. CBS licensed Fender Japan the right to build Fender guitars in Japan for the Japanese market. Fujigen, best known for its excellent Ibanez-brand instruments, was chosen as the factory.

Meanwhile in the States, the new management team were working on a strategy to return Fender to its former glory. The plan was, quite simply, for Fender to copy itself: to recreate those good old Fenders made back in the late 1950s and early 1960s.

The new team needed more information to assist in this proposed programme of re-creation. So Fender R&D man John Page travelled with Dan Smith to vintage-guitar dealer Ax In Hand in Illinois, where they took measurements and photographs and paint-tests from the relevant old Fenders.

"We left having bought perfect examples of each era," said Smith. "We spent $5,600 on a '57 Precision, '60 Jazz Bass, and a '61 Strat. Which for Fender at the time was ludicrous. We went out and bought back our own product."[66]

Such industry resulted in the Vintage reissue series. The basses consisted of a Vintage '62 Jazz Bass, a maple-neck anodised-pickguard Vintage '57 Precision Bass, and a rosewood-board tortoiseshell-guard Vintage '62 Precision Bass.

Production of the Vintage reissues was planned to start in 1982 at Fender U.S. (Fullerton) and at Fender Japan (Fujigen) but the changes being made at the American factory meant that the U.S. versions did not come on-stream until early 1983, and the factory there was not up to full speed until the start of '84. With variations on the model names, the '57 and '62 P-Basses and the '62 Jazz have been in production more or less continually since then. Pressure from Fender's European agents for cheaper models to compete with Japanese imports resulted in the birth of Fender's budget brand, Squier.

The name came from a string-making company, V.C. Squier of Michigan, that Fender had acquired in 1965. Victor Carroll Squier was born in 19th-century Boston, the son of an English immigrant, and became a violin maker, moving to Battle Creek, Michigan, where he founded his own shop with Gus Crawford in 1890 and developing a string-making business along the way. The company operated at the same Battle Creek building from 1927 to 1972, when CBS relocated the operation within the town. (Two Squier employees split from the company before the CBS sale to form the GHS string firm in the same town.)

Vintage-style Squier basses began to appear from Fender Japan in 1982. At first, export-to-Europe models were distinguished by the addition of a small 'Squier Series' logo on the tip of the headstock, but this was soon changed to a large 'Squier' that replaced the Fender logo.

The Squier brand marked the start of the sale of Fender Japan products around the world and the move by Fender to become an international manufacturer of guitars, and the logo soon spread to basses of modern as well as vintage designs. Fender themselves describe Squier as the 'value brand' alternative to its big brother.

At the U.S. factory in the early 1980s, two series of a Standard Jazz Bass and Standard Precision Bass appeared. In the second series, introduced in '83, cost-cutting meant that both gained a 'bullet' truss-rod adjuster at the headstock and the Jazz had a one-piece pickguard with all controls and the jack mounted on it. These odd varieties of Fender's key models were gone by the end of 1985.

Another shortlived Fender at the time was the Elite Precision, intended as a radical high-end version of the old faithful. It bravely tried to incorporate trends of the time like active electronics (first seen on a Fender on 1980's Precision Special), heavy brass hardware, and an improved truss-rod design. The Elite was a step forward for Fender, at the same time as the retro-looking Vintage models, but business uncertainties meant the line was dropped by 1985.

Bass on an eighties high

By the first few years of the 1980s, the bass guitar – whether it was made in the U.S.A., Japan, Europe, or elsewhere – had come of age. Since its birth some 30 years earlier, makers and musicians had ensured that the electric bass now had many new facilities that established the instrument more than ever as an essential part of contemporary music making.

■ Yamaha BB5000 1987
(main bass) One of the earliest production five-strings, the 5000 appeared in '84, a relatively affordable alternative to custom fives. Session star **Nathan East** (right) is a fan. Later, many players preferred fives with wider string spacing.

■ Ibanez Musician 1979
(below) This fretless bass belonged to **Sting** (seen with it on stage, right) who used it for a good deal of his Police work. Ibanez, along with Aria, redefined the image of Japanese basses in the late 1970s as well-made and fine sounding instruments, bringing many features of more expensive custom makers such as Alembic to a more affordable line of basses. Sting's melodic, thoughtful bass work was an underrated component of The Police (1977–83, and again more recently). He also used Fender basses, especially for later solo work, and Fender issued a signature Precision in 2001.

■ **Aria Pro II SB1000 1980**
(right) Issued in the late 70s, the SB1000 gave credibility to the work of Japanese bass makers. Its through-neck construction and active electronics are hallmarks of the period. A prominent Aria user was **John Taylor** (far right) of Duran Duran.

YAMAHA *BB5000*

Bassist Jeff Berlin summed up the focus on the bass guitar in a 1984 magazine column. "Look what's happening to the electric bass these days," he enthused. "The instrument is becoming more modernized all the time. They're building four-string, five-string, six-string, eight-string, fretless, piccolo, and two-octave basses; basses with thick necks, thin necks, and graphite necks, plastic bodies, wood bodies, no bodies; and every conceivable combination of strings, bridges, pickups, tone and volume controls (both active and passive), tuning pegs, strap locks, and even nut pieces."[67]

Clearly a revolution had taken place among musicians and manufacturers. The industry must have been delighted to see a boom in sales during the 1980s as the bass guitar became the hip instrument of the moment and a glut of successful bassists highlighted its new-found versatility and prominence.

In Europe it was Mark King who personified the fresh cult of the bass. As the talented bass-playing frontman for Level 42, who had a stream of Top-10 hits from 1984 onwards and were best heard on the *World Machine* album (1985), King at first played his funky slap style on a British Alembic-influenced Jaydee bass. He led a whole new generation of players to take up the evidently enjoyable and hugely fashionable bass guitar. Even the most non-musical individual was checking out this guy, who fronted his band while singing and slapping, and accordingly the bass guitar became identifiable as much more than just an instrument with a supporting role.

In the U.S.A. it was Billy Sheehan, who came to prominence in the pop-metal band of singer David Lee Roth, where he cheerfully battled it out with Roth's guitarist Steve Vai. A great slab of his work can be heard on Roth's *Eat 'Em And Smile* album (1986). Sheehan established himself from the mid 1980s onwards as a bass hero, much in the mould of the guitar hero of years past. His eccentrically modified Fender bass was marketed as the Attitude model by Yamaha, and Sheehan consistently topped popularity polls throughout the world by virtue of his accomplished playing skills and diligent self-promotion.

Pop fans and bass players alike were drawn to King and Sheehan, but few qualified more justifiably as the bassists' bassists of the decade than Marcus Miller and John Patitucci. While both men made worthy solo records, Miller applied the popular slap style to jazz most publicly on several recordings and tours of the tirelessly experimental trumpeter and bandleader Miles Davis – *Tutu* from 1986 is a fine example – using a modified Jazz Bass and, later, instruments by Sadowsky and Modulus.

Meanwhile, Patitucci's work on double bass and on six-string bass guitar (primarily a Ken Smith and later a Yamaha) was highlighted through his dates and sessions with jazz keyboardist Chick Corea, including the impressive *Inside Out* album (1990). And while we're still in the 1980s, be sure to check out some of the other great bassists prominent in that decade, from Geddy Lee's fine-detailed work in Rush and Cliff Burton's metal blueprint in Metallica, through two consistently inventive and melodic Brits, Mick Karn in Japan and Colin Moulding in XTC, and on to Louis Johnson's perfect bass for Michael Jackson's 'Billie Jean' (*Thriller*, 1982), Peter Hook's gritty Rickenbacker clank in Joy Division's 'Love Will Tear Us Apart' (1980), and Bakithi Kumalo's luscious fretless on Paul Simon's 'Diamonds On The Soles Of Her Shoes' (*Graceland*, 1986).

Fender for sale, would suit present owner

CBS decided during 1984 that they had finally had enough of the instrument business and wanted to sell Fender Musical Instruments. Mostly they blamed Japanese competition for Fender's recent losses. By the end of January 1985, almost exactly 20 years since they acquired it, CBS sold Fender to "an investor group led by William Schultz, president of Fender Musical Instruments". The sale was completed in March for $12.5 million.

With the hectic months of negotiations and financing behind them, Schultz and his team could now run Fender for themselves (and a number of investment banks). They faced many problems, but probably the most pressing was that the Fullerton factories were not included in the deal. So U.S. production of Fenders stopped in February 1985 – although the new team had been stockpiling bodies and necks and had acquired some existing inventory of completed guitars as well as production machinery. The company went from employing over 800 people in early 1984 down to just over 100 by early 1985.

Administration headquarters were established in Brea, California, not far from Fullerton. Six years later, Fender moved admin from Brea to Scottsdale, Arizona, where it remains today.

The new Japanese operation, established in 1982, became Fender's lifeline. All the guitars in Fender's 1985 catalogue were made in Japan, and probably as much as 80 percent of the instruments that Fender U.S. sold from around the end of 1984 to the middle of 1986 were Japanese.

Fender finally established their new U.S. factory at Corona, about 20 miles east of the defunct Fullerton site, in 1985. Dan Smith and his colleagues wanted to re-establish American production with a good, basic Precision Bass, Jazz Bass, Stratocaster, and Telecaster, which they hoped would be seen as a continuation of the best of Fender's long-standing American traditions. The guitar side sorted itself out quickly, translating into the new American Standard

■ **Fender Squier Vintage Series '62 Jazz 1982** (main bass) This Jazz Bass was one of the very first Squier Japanese Vintages off the line, with the small Squier logo ID. (Squier later became a brand for less expensive Fenders; see ad, above.) The bass is owned by Randy Hope-Taylor, who's worked with Jeff Beck and Incognito.

Fender's new dimension
Precision Bass Special.

Active
electronics
for active
bass players.

Fender

■ These ads (above) reveal the way Fender were thinking about the past and the present during the 1980s. The big idea of the moment was, in effect, for Fender to copy its classic basses. Setting up Fender Japan to make instruments outside the US, Fender offered a new line of 'vintage' copies of the great 50s and 60s basses, including this '57-style Precision (above left), complete with anodised-type pickguard. Absorbing current trends too, Fender offered the 1980 Precision Special (above right), with active electronics and heavy brass hardware, which at the time was thought to improve tone.

■ **Fender American Vintage '62 Precision Bass 1998** (right) With its Japanese factory up and running, Fender US joined in with 'vintage' re-creations. Basses from two classic eras were copied: the '57 style with fretted maple neck, and the '62 with rosewood board, like this more recent American Vintage bass.

111

Stratocaster (1986) and Telecaster (1988), but the story of the basses was trickier. Apart from the vintage models, there was no dead-on traditional-looking U.S.-made Fender Precision or Jazz Bass for about ten years from 1985.

Instead, the American Standard Jazz Bass of 1988 had 22 frets, unlike the traditional 20-fret Jazz, with the active 22-fret stack-knob Jazz Plus added a couple of years later. The 22-fret Precision Plus (1989) had a regular P-Bass pickup plus a bridge Jazz pickup. This so-called P/J layout was popular with some other makers, but this was its first appearance on a Fender. The Plus was followed by the similar Precision Plus Deluxe (1991), which was active and had two stack knobs. By 1995, sense prevailed once more and Fender offered an American-made model of each classic: the 20-fret passive American Standard Precision Bass and American Standard Jazz Bass (both renamed, dropping the 'Standard', in 2000, and then reverting to 'American Standard' in '08).

Fender began making offshore instruments in Korea as well as Japan. Some Squier models are still built there today (and some Fender-brand basses too) while the lowest-price Squiers are now usually produced in China, Indonesia, or India. In 1987, an additional Fender factory was established just across the California–Mexico border in Ensenada, Mexico, 180 miles south of Los Angeles. It was completely rebuilt after a devastating fire in 1994.

Back to (electric) acoustic

MTV, the music channel, started to broadcast a series in the late 1980s called *Unplugged*, capitalising on the rise in popularity of acoustic music at the time. The first *Unplugged* was broadcast in November 1989, featuring Squeeze and Elliot Easton of The Cars, and as more programmes followed, 'unplugged' quickly became a catchphrase that summed up a musical trend.

The idea of the show was that rock bands better known for loud, amplified work would unplug their electric equipment and play a concert with acoustic instruments. This proved surprisingly successful: many musicians clearly revelled in the opportunity to unplug and go acoustic, even if only for the one gig, and fans welcomed the appearance of a new slant on well-known material.

As far as the musical-instrument industry was concerned, the popularity of acoustic music in general and *Unplugged* in particular gave a new lease of life on the sales of acoustic instruments – and this is a trend that has never really gone away since.

Acoustic was in vogue, and air began to appear inside all manner of guitars – including basses. Consider for a moment an electric guitarist picking up a flat-top acoustic guitar. At that point he connects with a tradition that goes back at the very least to the Martin company's innovations early in the 20th century. But when the acoustic bass guitar first appeared in the 1970s it was a new hybrid instrument with no historical background, combining bass-guitar stringing and tuning with a flat-top acoustic guitar's construction.

Ironically, this initial combination only served to re-introduce one of the very problems the electric bass guitar had been designed to eliminate: that the inherent lack of volume of a pure acoustic instrument can only be increased by enlarging the size of the body, often to unmanageable proportions.

The huge dimensions of Mexico's established acoustic bass instrument, the guitarrón, inspired one of the earliest acoustic bass guitars, the big Earthwood Bass of 1972, built by the Ernie Ball company in California. Other acoustic bass guitars followed in the 1970s, including models made by Guild in the U.S.A. and Eko in Italy. In order to increase the volume of these hybrids, both companies offered optional versions with bridge-mounted pickups to provide a novel amplified-acoustic sound.

It was primarily this type of acoustic-electric bass that became popular as the *Unplugged* acoustic boom began to reverberate around the late 1980s – when 'acoustic' often meant acoustic only in looks and feel, because in reality amplification still had to be used to project most performances. The new breed of basses had thin bodies and bridge pickups, and the first to appear was the Kramer Ferrington in 1986.

Guitar-maker Danny Ferrington was a custom-builder who in the mid 1980s struck a licensing deal with the Kramer guitar company of New Jersey, who were looking for acoustic designs to sell to their decidedly electric clientele. First up was an acoustic-electric guitar in 1985, followed by a bass the following year. "They had standard electric-style necks on a thin acoustic body," Ferrington remembers of the Kramer Ferrington pointed-headstock models. "It was Kramer's way of getting to electric players, because acoustic was getting big then, but some players still thought you had to be a folkie or something. So I thought: make it small and slim, with the same access and feel as an electric bass." And that's exactly what he did.

The Kramer Ferrington debuted at the U.S. NAMM instrument show early in 1986. Ferrington: "We were the first with a thin acoustic bass with a pickup that you could play like a bass guitar. By the June show, Washburn had one, and by the following year everyone seemed to have them. Fleetwood Mac and Aerosmith used ours on video, and The Cure used it on their *Unplugged* show, because it looked a bit different from the ordinary."[68]

Most makers of modern acoustic-electric basses use piezo-electric pickups

■ **Fender Jazz Bass 1977**
This is Marcus Miller's bass,
modified to his requirements
by guitar maker Roger
Sadowsky. Miller is seen
using the bass on stage in
the picture (above). Fender
issued a signature edition in
1998 replicating this original.

■ **Marcus Miller** (opposite) is best known for his work with jazz legend Miles Davis on albums such as Tutu (1986) and Amandla (1989). He helped to bring modern playing techniques like slapping to jazz-rock. Another key player from the period is **John Patitucci** (below, with Ken Smith bass). Patitucci is a virtuoso on six-string bass, probably heard to best effect during his time with jazz keyboardist Chick Corea, including the album Inside Out (1990).

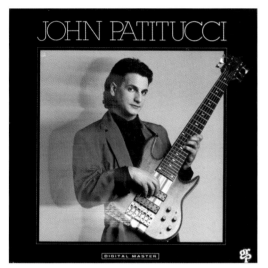

JOHN PATITUCCI

DIGITAL MASTER

■ Bass guitar came into its own during the 1980s as the instrument almost everyone seemed to want to play. Part of the attraction was the fame achieved by some prominent bass men, such as **Mark King** (above), of British pop-funk band Level 42, seen here with a Jaydee bass. In the USA it was Billy Sheehan of David Lee Roth's band who led the charge. Another formidable talent was **Cliff Burton** of Metallica (top, with trusty Rickenbacker), but he died tragically young in 1986.

mounted into the instrument's bridge, a system that had been established by Ovation around 1970. These pickups have special crystals that generate electricity under mechanical strain and, as a result, pick up the vibrations of the guitar's top as well as the individual strings.

The sound produced by a piezo-electric pickup is therefore different from that generated by a regular electric bass guitar's magnetic pickup, which responds solely to metal strings moving in its magnetic field. In theory at least, the piezo should give more 'acoustic' character in its amplified sound.

One of the attractions of an acoustic-electric bass is that it provides bass guitarists with the opportunity of obtaining something approaching a double bass sound. A closer approximation was achieved by the Ashbory bass (at one time produced by Guild and now by Fender), which featured rubber strings stretched over a tiny 22-inch scale, and a piezo pickup. In the hands of players such as Doug Wimbish and Tony Levin, the odd-looking Ashbory produced a remarkably convincing double bass emulation, all the more strange given its small size.

The art of synth bass

In sharp contrast to the acoustic trend, some manufacturers tried to link together the bass guitar and the synthesiser during the 1980s to make a new electronic instrument, the bass guitar synth. It was not an entirely new idea to try to make a bass sound like a keyboard: British maker Vox had developed a daring if unreliable Guitar Organ in the mid 1960s and made at least one prototype bass version.

Keyboard synthesisers had evolved quickly during the 1970s, and bassists looked on as synth players increasingly supplied basslines, especially on dance music recordings. Stevie Wonder was an early pioneer, in collaboration with his synth technicians Robert Margouleff and Malcolm Cecil, with big hits like 'Superstition' (1972) and the remarkable 'Boogie On Reggae Woman' (1974). More early and influential keyboard/sequencer-synth basslines came with two key records from 1977, Giorgio Moroder's 'I Feel Love' single, with vocalist Donna Summer, and Kraftwerk's *Trans-Europe Express* album. Also that year, David Bowie's *"Heroes"* album balanced to great effect George Murray's funky bass guitar and Brian Eno's mechanised synth worlds.

Some guitar makers saw the possibility of applying synthesiser technology to existing instruments. Ampeg's Patch 2000 was an early guitar synth, but it was Roland, a leading Japanese synthesiser manufacturer established in 1974, who did most to try to bring the bass-guitar synth to market. They began experiments in the late 1970s, developing the concept of a special guitar (the 'controller') plus a separate box containing most of the synthesiser circuitry.

Two early Roland bass systems appeared: the relatively conventional-looking G-33 or G-88 (1980) and the futuristic G-77 (1985), which had an angular body and a plastic neck-strengthening spar running parallel to the neck. The bass guitars were made for Roland by Fuji Gen-Gakki, known for some Ibanez and Fender/Squier basses.

Roland maintained faith in the idea. For many years the company developed its bass synth and tried to create a market – while no other manufacturers seemed confident or even interested enough to provide any competition. Bass players were in general unconvinced by the Roland, largely due to its inherent inability to immediately identify and reproduce all notes accurately.

One bassist who bravely used a Roland bass synth to 'play' sampled digital sounds was Dave Bronze, who has played bass with Robin Trower and Eric Clapton. He used a G-77 with British sampling pioneers The Art Of Noise on a 1986 tour. To counter the delay inherent in Roland's system, particularly in the lower register, Bronze transposed the bass samples down an octave and played everything up an octave, which reduced the problem.

"We just about got away with it," he laughs. "The odd thing was that after doing that eight-week world tour, when I went back to normal bass I found I was playing ahead of the beat all the time. I had to work with a metronome and learn to play on or behind the beat again."[69]

Most players were not willing to make such compromises in order to achieve sounds that could be made much more easily and reliably with keyboard instruments, and the Rolands faded from the scene.

Later experiments led to Steve Chick's MIDI Bass system, incorporated into basses by makers such as Wal in England and Valley Arts in the U.S.A., and prompted the Peavey Midibase and CyberBass models of the early 1990s.

None lasted, and the bass-guitar synth was another idea that faded into history. Recent developments with digital modelling, of which more later, have since provided a revised modern version of the electronic bass guitar.

Fender bass: engrained in our DNA

John Page and Michael Stevens started Fender's Custom Shop in January 1987. One of the first instruments they made was a '62 Precision Bass in 'Mary Kaye' style, with blond body and gold-plated hardware. The order was placed in mid May 1987 and Page completed the instrument on June 22nd.

The expansion of the Custom Shop's business prompted a move in 1993 to

■ **Martin B-65 1990** (above);
Guild Ashbory 1987 (below)
Martin, best known for their
acoustic flat-tops, joined the
acoustic-electric bass trend
with typcially understated flair.
The Ashbory is a tiny 22-inch-
scale bass with rubber strings
that produces a remarkably
good double-bass sound.

■ Washburn's modern products are mostly of US design and oriental manufacture and include acoustic-electric basses. These were popularised during the boom in acoustic music, highlighted by MTV's Unplugged series of shows that began in the late 1980s. The key to the sound was a piezo pickup in the bridge, designed to give more acoustic vibe than a regular magnetic pickup. Washburn's ad from 1991 (right) features a number of piezo-bass players. Meanwhile, some bassists rebelled against the technological developments of the era and went in the opposite direction – like **Mark Sandman** (above) of Morphine and his two-string vintage Premier bass.

■ **Fender Precision Plus 1990** (main bass) More fiddling by Fender, who couldn't decide what a modern Precision should be at the time. This one has the first appearance on a Fender of the 'P and J' pickup layout, with modified controls to match. The body has been skewed too, with an elongated upper horn. Only later in the 90s did matters settle down.

new buildings – still close to the Corona factory – providing extra space and improved efficiency. When Fender's new plant was unveiled five years later, the Custom Shop was at last shifted into the factory. At the start of the 1990s, the Shop had built about 2,500 guitars a year, and by 1996 that figure had risen to some 7,000 instruments annually – most of which are, of course, six-string Strats and Teles. Fender will not discuss current numbers, but it's safe to assume that they have climbed dramatically.

Fender reorganised models into new series in the late 1990s, around the time the company established that new factory, still in Corona, California. Today, the list of regular factory basses features high-end U.S.-made 'modern' models grouped as American Deluxes and reissues brought together as American Vintages. Highway One models combine modern features and vintage styling, building on the classic vibe of the American Standard series. Less expensive models from Fender's various overseas manufacturing plants (including Mexico) are grouped into the Classic, Deluxe, and Standard series.

There were some newer ideas among the retro and modernised retro: the Jazz Bass 24 is an affordable Korean-made 24-fret Jazz while the Jaguar Bass is a Japanese-made combination of Jaguar guitar and Jazz Bass. Signature models usually now reside in the Artist Series, ranging from the simple Sting Precision to Marcus Miller's personalised active Jazz, from Stu Hamm's unusual Urge Bass (which in 1993 had been the first Fender signature bass) to Geddy Lee's '70s-vibe Jazz.

There's been a recent move to a stronger emphasis on the bass at Fender. In 2002, a bass-specific team was set up within the marketing department, at first concentrating on bass amps and then shifting to include the bass guitars. This explains some of the recent developments, underlined by Jay Piccirillo, who is Senior Marketing Manager for Fender and Squier bass products.

"The Precision and Jazz Bass platforms will live on as *the* sound of bass," says Piccirillo, "engrained in the DNA of our culture. When you hear electric bass, you hear Fender.

"I think we have a lot of great basses ahead of us," he continues. "We have bass-playing employees all over the world who are jumping at the chance to help bring bass to the forefront. Think about this: we are a giant in the bass guitar world, yet still only a small component of Fender Musical Instruments Corp. We have always given basses respect and attention, but the level of focus and support now in place will allow us to really take things up a level."[70]

Fender have attempted to wipe out straight copies of their basses by establishing the Japanese company and producing there and elsewhere good lower-priced versions of the best-known models. In recent years, too, the company has actively defended its trademarks for model names and headstock shapes, and is also investigating its trademark rights for body shapes.

Some makers influenced by Fender have made an impression at the high-end of the market. One such is Lakland, founded by Dan Lakin and Hugh McFarland in Chicago in 1995. Lakin told an interviewer that the first Lakland was "sort of Leo Fender's greatest hits – a J-Bass and an early Music Man StingRay put together".[71]

Lakland's instruments today include signature models based on the instruments of revered session men Joe Osborn (his old Jazz Bass) and Duck Dunn (his old Precision) and Rolling Stones man Darryl Jones (a sort of shifted Jazz). Of course, like any intelligent maker, Lakland brings fresh approaches of its own and new ideas, such as the Hollowbody and Decade models. But it's the ghosts of Leo and his teams who justifiably loom strongly in the background of this and many other modern bass producers.

Warwick and the sound of wood

Hans-Peter Wilfer set up Warwick in Erlangen, near Nuremburg, Germany in 1982 and gradually through the decades has turned it into a leading bass name, helped by distinctive instruments and strong endorsers to its current position among the top international bass brands.

Wilfer had started working at the Framus guitar company when he was just 17 – helped by the fact that his father, Fred Wilfer, owned the company. Fred had founded Framus in 1946 and it became a key European player in the guitar boom of the 1960s. One of Bill Wyman's early instruments was a Framus Star Bass. Success was harder to find later, and Framus limped on before closing in 1981. Hans-Peter was determined to create a new company himself.

He chose a non-German sounding brandname, Warwick, and at first wasn't clear if he would make guitars, basses, or both. At his debut Frankfurt trade fair in the early 1980s he showed a Stratocaster and a Flying V with their Fender and Gibson logos switched to Warwick, plus a proper Warwick bass, the Nobby Meidel headless model, named for a local musician and influenced by the then-fashionable Steinberger.

"I didn't sell anything else at that show other than, I think, 25 Nobby Meidel basses," Wilfer recalls. "And so because we were just a small workshop then, with two people plus me and my mother, I decided to concentrate on basses. It seemed there was more market potential there."

The next two models, the Streamer (1984) and the Thumb (1985), defined

■ **Roland G-77 1985** (main bass) Synthesisers invaded some of the bass player's space in the 1970s and into the 80s. At first it was keyboard synths that provided the key weapons of the battle. Stevie Wonder showed what could be done with synth bass, and dance producer **Giorgio Moroder** (right) provided a key lesson in mechanised bass lines with the records he created for the likes of Donna Summer. Then along came Japanese synth giant Roland, who attempted to make a piece of kit with a bass guitar controlling a synth unit. The G-77 pictured was a striking example but suffered, like other similar efforts, from poor 'tracking' of notes. It did not last long.

■ Fender continued its old versus new debate into the 90s. Achievements included the first five-string Fender, the **Jazz Plus V** (opposite) of 1990, and the company's first signature bass, the 1995 **Stu Hamm Urge** (right). Meanwhile, in 1996 Fender celebrated 50 years of existence, as this ad (left) with prominent vintage-style Precision and Jazz testifies.

50 years

Fifty years ago, Fender started a revolution that would change the course of modern music forever. Four of their remarkable instruments have gone on to become standards by which all others are judged. The Stratocaster, Telecaster, Precision Bass and Jazz Bass are arguably the world's most copied instruments. Imitated but never equalled.

1996 is Fender's 50th Anniversary. As part of the celebrations, it seems only fitting to pay tribute to those instruments that have

played a pivotal role in creating the sound of contemporary music. In honour of this, we introduce the American Standard 50th Anniversary Limited Editions.

Exclusive features of these once in a lifetime instruments include: gold plated American Standard hardware, highly figured maple veneer top and back, Antique Sunburst finish, vintage pickups and electronics and a black tolex vintage case with plush interior and vintage Fender nameplate.

These superb instruments are sure to become sought-after collectors items in years to come, and production is strictly limited. Try a piece of Fender's history at your dealer now.

Fender

Distributed exclusively by ARBITER GROUP PLC Wilberforce Road, London NW9 6AX Tel: 0181 202 1199 Fax: 0181 202 7076 Web site at: http://www.demon.co.uk/arbiter

the classic Warwick look and construction. These basses were made using beautiful exotic woods, with a laminated through-neck, Warwick's trademark angled-back tuners, active pickups, and a luxurious vibe. They had a gently curved body, arched on the top and concave on the back. This, admits Wilfer, was copied from Spector basses of the day. A shortlived license deal was made with Spector soon afterward.

The name of the Thumb bass underlined its appeal to the slapping bassists of the 1980s, and as a relatively small-bodied instrument it was designed to work sitting high on the player's body. The lovely natural hardwoods that Warwick use – bubinga, afzelia, flamed maple, zebrano, swamp ash, ovangkol, wenge, and others – gave the instruments an attractive glow among the epoxy'd fare from Steinberger and others. "The Thumb bass was completely modern, but went back to the retro feel of old wood," says Wilfer.

Other models have followed, including the more dramatically shaped Dolphin and Vampyre, and the successful Corvette, but it's been Warwick's close association with key players that explains some of its success. "All artists are important," says Wilfer. "Our audience have heroes and their heroes are the artists. The two most important for our company have been John Entwistle and Jack Bruce. Everyone who thinks of Jack Bruce today thinks first of a Warwick and second of a Gibson bass."

Wilfer recalls Entwistle coming on to the Warwick booth at a trade show in the early 1980s. "Somebody told me that is John Entwistle from The Who. And I said from who? They were never a big act for me when I was 18, I was more into disco. Let's be fair: a lot of artists who are really big and respected now didn't mean a thing in the early 1980s. It seems today that older acts are almost as important as younger acts."

Wilfer and Entwistle stayed in touch, and it led to the design of the Warwick Buzzard, which Entwistle used on stage with The Who in the late 1980s (and which also appeared in a graphite version by British maker Status).

In 1995, Warwick moved to Markneukirchen in the old East Germany (the same town that effectively marked the birth of Martin acoustic guitars many years earlier). Wilfer started afresh with new machines and new workers. He says it took a few years in order to get back up to speed, but today he is happy with Warwick's new situation and their success internationally. Another recent move was to manufacture a new line of basses in China with the Rockbass By Warwick brand, although the hard-working Wilfer plans within five years to bring that production back to Europe. "It is a lifetime job,"[72] says Wilfer as he considers what appears to be a rosy future for Warwick and its players.

Model that bass

The 1990s saw many bass players redefining their art. To generalise, the complicated was put aside and retro was the flavour of the decade – although, as ever, all kinds of exceptions confound that and any other trend you care to name.

Just listen to some of the variety on offer in what's almost a random list: from Mike Chapman with Garth Brooks (*Ropin' The Wind*, 1991) to Victor Wooten with Bela Fleck & The Flecktones (*Live Art*, 1996), John Ciambotti with Lucinda Williams (*Car Wheels On A Gravel Road*, 1998) to Les Claypool with Primus (*Sailing The Seas Of Cheese*, 1991), and Stuart Zender with Jamiroquai (*Emergency On Planet Earth*, 1993) to Flea with The Red Hot Chili Peppers (*One Hot Minute*, 1995).

Digital modelling was a new idea as players entered the 21st century. The idea is to make available digital samples of classic instrument and amp sounds. California-based Line 6 were the leaders, and their Bass Pod bass amp modeller box of 2000 showed what could be done. They launched a modelling bass guitar, the Variax Bass 700, in 2004, with the five-string 705 following a year later.

Line 6's Variax basses contained stored digital models of vintage and modern electric basses as well as acoustic upright and synth-bass tones, providing what the maker called "instant access to sounds never before available in a single instrument". There were 24 digitally modelled sounds onboard, ranging from the expected vintage Fenders through Music Man StringRay, Rick 4001, Hofner violin, Gibson Thunderbird, Warwick Thumb, and Modulus Flea, and on to Danelectro, Alembic, Steinberger, and others.

Some players welcomed such apparent diversity in one instrument; others pointed to the importance of the playability and feel of an individual bass beyond the isolated constituents of sound and tone. The Variax basses didn't last long. Fender has already come up with a modelling guitar, the Stratocaster VG, so perhaps they'll chance a modelling Fender bass too.

A rather more physical trend among a handful of players and makers was a move beyond the well established five-string bass and the more specialist six-string bass. Conklin, for example, was established by Bill Conklin in 1984 in Missouri, and they make seven, eight, and nine-string custom options for their basses, and even delivered a custom-ordered 11-string bass. Correct: eleven strings. Can this still be considered a bass guitar? We think not.

Old, vintage, or new?

For bass players, the idea of 'vintage' instruments turned up later than for guitarists. Since the 1970s, guitar players have generally revered and desired old

■ **Peavey Cirrus 5 2006** (above); **Warwick Thumb 1993** (below); **Lakland 5594 USA Classic 1999** (right) Some examples of the modern bass maker's art here. Peavey's Cirrus line combines classic features and modern playability. The other two basses have famous names attached: the Warwick belongs to Jack Bruce, while the custom Lakland was owned by ex-Bad Company bassist Boz Burrell, who died in 2006.

■ **Warwick Corvette Double-Buck five-string 2008** (below) German maker Warwick has become known for exotic woods and distinctive designs, exemplified by the Corvette line.

■ **James LoMenzo** of Megadeth is seen on stage in 2007 (above) with his Warwick Buzzard. "People call me a wuss because I only bring two basses on tour, but I only play one a night," said LoMenzo of his straightforward approach. "We don't experiment with any strange tunings or anything like that so there's really not much need to change them over."

127

instruments, primarily from the classic 1950s and '60s periods and also now from the 1970s. Bass players instead found themselves seduced by upscale handmade basses, or instruments in that style, inspired by the work of Alembic and others.

But the retro return-to-the-roots craze has been in place since the 1990s, and this in essence has meant grabbing an old Fender or Fender-style bass and laying down the groove – confirming, extraordinarily, that Leo Fender and his team pretty much got the design right in the early years of the instrument's development. This notion of absorbing the best factors that made past instruments so distinctive and catching a bonus from the fashionable retro vibe meant that Fender was perfectly placed to exploit the trend.

We've seen how Fender began its own programme of reissuing basses from the original periods in order to replicate the look and build and, ideally, the playability of those original designs. They began half-heartedly with the Telecaster Bass in 1968 and then properly in the early 1980s with the Vintage series '57 and '62 Precision and '62 Jazz.

More recently these have become the bass arm of the American Vintage series, with the addition of a '75 Jazz Bass (in period natural-finish body plus block markers) and a few others from the Custom Shop. There's also now the newer and less expensive Classic Series ('51 and 50s P-Bass, 60s Jazz, and Mustang), while a retro vibe is evident in many other current Fender lines.

In the '90s, Fender came up with an interesting twist. The idea was to 'age' brand new guitars to look like vintage oldies. The story goes, according to a Fender insider, that Keith Richards asked Fender's Custom Shop to "bash up" some replica guitars they'd made for him for a Stones tour.

So the Shop began to include wear-and-tear distress marks to replicate the overall look of a battered old original. Fender's 'new oldies', known as Relics, took off, at first with guitars. By 1996, a Relic Jazz Bass had been added to the line, an idea continued independently by German maker Sandberg.

Today there are three strands of these 're-creations' in what Fender now calls its Time Machine series, made in the company's Custom Shop.

There's the original Relic style, given 'aged' knocks and the look of heavy wear, as if the bass has been out on the road for a generation or so. The Closet Classics are made to look like they were bought new way back when, played a few times, and then stuck in a closet. The N.O.S., or 'New Old Stock', basses are supposed to look as if an instrument had been bought brand new in the 1950s or 1960s and then put straight into a time machine that transported it to the present day.

The Time Machine models are a brilliant move by Fender, the nearest they've come with new instruments to the almost indefinable appeal of vintage basses. Many had thought that this magical quality was like the specific blue used in medieval stained glass: something permanently and irretrievably lost in the past. Some still do.

By 2008, the Custom Shop's Time Machine series included two basses, a '59 Precision and a '64 Jazz.

Both were available in each of the three levels of aging – Relic, Closet Classic, or N.O.S. – and the list-prices hovered around $3,500. This might seem high, but when you compare what you might have to pay today for those now highly collectable originals – from maybe $20,000 for a blond '59 P-Bass with anodised 'guard to possibly $25,000 for a '64 Olympic White Jazz – then the attraction becomes clearer.

The next best bassline

As we've learned, for almost ten years from the bass guitar's launch in 1951, manufacturers were unconvinced that it had commercial potential. Many had trouble deciding whether or not to produce one.

And even if they did, recording engineers and band leaders hesitated to use it, and musicians weren't sure if it was an instrument to be taken up by double bass players or guitarists. All of them would surely have been amazed if they knew how much original-period basses sell for today. They might even have stashed a few away.

But with the dramatic explosion of pop music in the early 1960s, the task of deciding who *would* play this unfashionable background instrument rapidly developed into who *could* play the alternative styles and demanding techniques of later years.

The development of the instrument has been led by players. In recent years, many good bassists have ensured the healthy, continuing story of great bass, from the simplest root line to the most complicated finger-fest. No doubt you have your own current favourites, so (for once) we won't bore you with ours.

And despite all the ideas and all the improvements and changes over the years that we've covered in these pages, still the main trend at the time of writing is retro: in other words, the idea of going back and drawing upon the original designs of Fender and Fender-style instruments. It is remarkable to consider that Leo Fender and his team got so much so right so early.

The bass guitar is an irreplaceable part of modern music – and, we have no doubt, will always remain so. We are one nation under a groove.

■ **Fender Time Machine '59 Precision Bass 2008** (main bass, below) If anything is emblematic of the recent bass vibe, it has to be simplicity and retro. Not to say that the playing can't be complex, in the right circumstances, but the move to straightforward basses has been obvious for some time. Even players such as **Victor Wooten** (left) opt for simpler tools, like the custom Fodera Yin Yang four-string he's seen with here. Fender is in a prime spot to benefit from the retro fashion, and offers a crowded line of vintage-style models, at the top of which sits the Custom Shop Time Machine replicas, like this lovely N.O.S. ('new old stock') P-Bass. A recent catalogue (left) accentuates the wide range of players still drawn to the classic instrument's inventor.

■ **Line 6 Variax five-string 2005** (above) An update of the synth-bass idea came with digital modelling, pioneered by Line 6. But this Variax modelling bass, with on-board samples of all the classic bass sounds you might need, was dropped after a few years. Perhaps this is another indication of many players' preference for simple, direct instruments. **Flea** (above) of the Red Hot Chili Peppers seems content with his no-frills Modulus and its personal touches.

FOOTNOTES

1 Interview with the authors, November 30th 1994

2 Rickenbacker catalogue circa 1938

3 Regal catalogue #9 circa 1938–39

4 Vega catalogue #33 circa 1938

5 Gibson catalogue 1928

6 *Guitar Player* May 1978

7 *Rolling Stone* February 12th 1976

8 *Bay Area Music* August 29th 1980

9 Bill Carson in correspondence with Tony Bacon, September 6th 1991

10 Interview with the authors, November 29th 1994

11 Klaus Blasquiz *The Fender Bass* (Hal Leonard undated)

12 *The Music Trades* April 1952

13 Willie G. Moseley *Stellas & Stratocasters* (Vintage Guitar Books 1994)

14 Interview with the authors, November 29th 1994

15 Interview with Tony Bacon, February 8th 1992

16 Interview with Tony Bacon, February 5th 1992

17 *The Music Trades* August 1952

18 *Down Beat* July 30th 1952

19 Interview with the authors, November 29th 1994

20 *Melody Maker* September 12th 1953

21 *Melody Maker* October 17th 1953

22 *Melody Maker* November 14th 1953

23 *Melody Maker* November 28th 1953

24 Interview with Maggie Hawthorn, 1980

25 *The Music Trades* December 1957

26 Danelectro catalogue 1956

27 Interview with the authors, November 30th 1994

28 *The Music Trades* July 1961

29 Dave Marsh *Before I Get Old: The Story Of The Who* (Plexus 1989)

30 Peter Guralnick *Last Train To Memphis: The Rise Of Elvis Presley* (Little, Brown 1994)

31 Interview with Tony Bacon, November 15th 2007

32 *Popular Music And Society* October 2003

33 *Guitar Player* November 1994

34 U.S. Patent Office *Electromagnetic Pickup For Lute-Type Musical Instrument* January 9, 1959

35 *The Music Trades* August 1957

36 Interview with the authors, November 29th 1994

37 Interview with the authors, November 29th 1994

38 *The Music Trades* April 1957

39 http://www.provide.net/%7Ecfh/fenderc.html

40 Interview with Tony Bacon, February 8th 1992

41 Interview with the authors, November 30th 1994

42 *The Record Producers* BBC Radio 2, August 27th 2007

43 Dr. Licks (Allan Slutsky) *Standing In The Shadows Of Motown: The Life And Music Of Legendary Bassist James Jamerson* (Dr. Licks 1989)

44 Interview with the authors, November 30th 1994

45 Interview with Tony Bacon, February 10th 1992

46 *The Music Trades* February 1968

47 Interview with the authors, December 1st 1994

48 Rick Turner interview with the authors, December 7th 1994

49 *Rolling Stone* Audio Supplement September 27th 1973

50 Interview with the authors, December 7th 1994

51 *Guitar Player* May 1980

52 Interview with the authors, November 30th 1994

53 Interview with the authors, December 1st 1994

54 Interview with the authors, December 7th 1994

55 Interview with the authors, December 1st 1994

56 Interview with the authors, November 30th 1994

57 Interview with the authors, November 30th 1994

58 Interview with the authors, November 30th 1994

59 Interview with the authors, December 1st 1994

60 *The Music Trades* December 1971

61 Bill Wyman *Rolling With The Stones* (Dorling Kindersley 2002)

62 Interview with Tony Bacon, January 4th 1995

63 Interview with Tony Bacon, July 28th 1976

64 *Musician* December 1987

65 *Guitar Player* May 1978

66 Interview with Tony Bacon, February 4th 1992

67 *Guitar Player* March 1994

68 Interview with the authors, January 9th 1995

69 Interview with Tony Bacon, May 5th 1994

70 Interview with Tony Bacon, November 20th 2007

71 *Bass Player* January 2000

72 Interview with Tony Bacon, November 19th 2007

reference section

Reference Section

This part of The Bass Book uses a simple condensed format to convey a large amount of information about the bass guitars produced by 16 brands, with an emphasis on Fender basses. These notes are designed to help you get the most from this unique inventory.

We have included as many key bass brands as possible, with Fender and Squier given comprehensive coverage, listing every Jazz and Precision model. The other 14 manufacturers, from Alembic to Yamaha, are provided with entries covering selected principal models. Each maker's entry, including Fender, also features a brief list of various other bass models they have produced. (If you can't find a company or brand here, try checking the index at the back; this may link you to a reference elsewhere in the book.)

The company's **brandname** appears at the head of the listing, followed by a **country** or countries of origin, and then the individual entries, in alphabetical order (with a few noted exceptions) of model name.

At the head of each entry is the **model name** in bold type. Please be aware that we have not included the word 'Bass' in any model names, to avoid constant repetition. (This is *The Bass Book*, after all.) The model name is followed by a date or **range of dates** showing the known production period of the instrument. A range of dates (for example, 1982–94) indicates the start year and finish year. A start year with a dash (for example 1998–) means that production has ceased but the finish date is not known. A start year followed by a dash and 'current' (for example 2001–current) confirms the model was still in production at the time of writing. All dates are as accurate as possible but must still be considered approximate, because there is no foolproof method to pinpoint precise production years of any instrument.

In italic type following the model name and dates is a brief one-sentence **identification** of the bass in question, which should help you tell that model apart from others made by the same company. For some basses there may also be a sentence below this, reading "Similar to … except …". This will refer you to another model entry, and the accompanying description will outline any major differences between the two.

In most major entries there will next be a list of **specification points**, separated into groups and providing details of the model's features. In the order listed, these points may refer to:

- Neck, fingerboard, position markers, scale length, frets or fret markers, headstock, tuner layout.
- Body, finish.
- Pickup(s).
- Controls, jack socket location. (American readers may know the jack socket simply as the jack.)
- Pickguard.
- Bridge, tailpiece.
- Hardware finish.
- Special features (if any).

Some models were/are made in a number of **variations**, and where applicable these have been listed after the specification points, in italic type, along with any other general comments.

A model may have only a short entry, all in italic type. This is usually because it is a **reissue** of, or a re-creation based on, an earlier bass. The text will usually refer you to the entry for the original instrument.

Selected **additional basses** made by a company are grouped at the end of that maker's entry under the heading "Other basses produced by ... include ...".

Because of their size and scope, the **Fender** and **Squier** sections have some differences to the others. The Fender section opens with a list of features considered common to all its basses, to avoid repetition in the entries, and Squier does the same individually for Jazz models and Precision models.

Please note, again, that the word 'Bass' has not been included in model names, because we want to reduce unnecessary repetition. Throughout the Fender and Squier sections, 'Precision Bass' is always termed Precision and 'Jazz Bass' simply Jazz, along with all the permutations of model terminology (for example, American Classic Jazz, not American Classic Jazz Bass, '62 Precision Limited Edition rather than '62 Precision Bass Limited Edition, and so on).

The Fender section is split into three levels. First, there is a division by place of manufacture (U.S., Mexico, Japan, and Korea, in that order). Within those divisions, there are headings for Jazz, Precision, and Other Models. Then, within the U.S., Mexico, and Japan Jazz and Precision listings, models are further separated into what we have called Regular, Replica, and Revised models. The Fender section also features a basic guide to dating by serial number.

The information for all the brands and models here has been gathered through lengthy and detailed research. The listings do not pretend to list every bass guitar ever made – that would take a whole shelf of rather boring books – but are intended to act as guides to the specs and production histories of some of the instruments that you might come across regularly. We welcome any updates to the information shown – contact details can be found at the front and at the back of the book.

ALEMBIC

U.S.

SERIES I 1971–current *Double-cutaway body, centre dummy pickup, four controls.*

- Through-neck with ebony fingerboard, oval markers; 34–inch scale, 24 frets; truss-rod adjuster at body end; two-a-side tuners with metal keys.
- Semi-solid double-cutaway body; natural only.
- Two black plain pickups plus centre hum-cancelling unit.
- Four controls (two volume, two tone), rotary selector and two tone mini-switches all on body; front-mounted jack socket and XLR socket; active circuit with outboard power supply.
- Four-saddle bridge, tailpiece.

Various string, scale, style, construction and colour options.

SERIES II 1971–current *Double-cutaway body, centre dummy pickup, five controls.*

- Through-neck with ebony fingerboard, oval markers; 34–inch scale, 24 frets; truss-rod adjuster at body end; two-a-side tuners with metal keys.
- Semi-solid double-cutaway body; natural only.
- Two black plain pickups plus centre hum-cancelling unit.
- Five controls (three volume, two tone), rotary selector and two tone rotary switches, all on body; front-mounted jack socket and XLR socket; active circuit with outboard power supply.
- Four-saddle bridge, tailpiece.

Various string, scale, style, construction and colour options.

STANLEY CLARKE SIGNATURE DELUXE

1988–current *Signature on headstock, twin-cutaway mahogany & rosewood body.*

- Through-neck with ebony fingerboard, oval markers; 30.75–inch scale, 24 frets; truss-rod adjuster at body end; two-a-side tuners with metal keys; Stanley Clarke signature on headstock.
- Solid twin-cutaway body; natural only.
- Two black plain pickups.
- Four controls (volume, two tone, balance) and two tone mini-switches, all on body; front-mounted jack socket; active circuit.
- Four-saddle bridge, tailpiece.

Various string, style, construction and colour options. Also STANLEY CLARKE SIGNATURE STANDARD (1990–current).

Other basses produced by Alembic include:
Distillate 1978–90
Epic 1993–current
Essence 1991–current
Europa 1986–current
Excel 1998–current
Mark King Signature Deluxe 1988–current
Mark King Signature Standard 1990–current
Persuader 1983–
Rogue 1997–current
Spoiler 1980–94
20th Anniversary 1989

ARIA PRO II

Japan

SB-1000 first version 1979–87 *Through-neck, solid contoured double-cutaway body, one pickup, two controls, six-way rotary selector, mini-switch.*

- Through-neck with rosewood fingerboard (ebony from c1982), dot markers; 34–inch scale, 24 frets; truss-rod adjuster at headstock end; two-a-side tuners with metal keys.
- Solid contoured double-cutaway body; natural only.
- One black plain pickup.
- Two controls (volume, tone), six-way rotary selector and mini-switch, all on body; front-mounted jack socket; active circuit.
- Four-saddle bridge/tailpiece.

SB-1000 second version 1990–93 *Through-neck, solid contoured double-cutaway body, two pickups, three controls.*

- Through-neck with rosewood fingerboard, dot markers; 34–inch scale, 24 frets; truss-rod adjuster at headstock end; two-a-side tuners with metal keys.
- Solid contoured double-cutaway body; black or natural.
- Two black plain pickups.
- Three controls (two volume, one tone), all on body; side-mounted jack socket.
- Four-saddle bridge/tailpiece.
- Gold-plated hardware.

SB-1000RI 1994–current *Reissue based on SB-1000 first version (see earlier listing).*

Other basses produced by Aria include:
Avante series 1992–current
Integra series 1986–current
Magna series 1990–
RS series 1983–
SB series 1979–current

DANELECTRO

U.S.

LONG HORN model 4423 1958–69 *Slab body with twin long outward curving horns.*
- Bolt-on neck with rosewood fingerboard, dot markers; 33.5–inch scale, 24 frets; no truss-rod adjuster; two-a-side tuners with metal or plastic keys.
- Semi-solid slab twin-cutaway body, long outward curving horns; sunburst only.
- Two metal-cover tubular pickups.
- Two dual-concentric controls (each volume/on-off) on body; side-mounted jack socket.
- Clear plastic pickguard.
- Single-saddle bridge/tailpiece.

Korea

58 LONGHORN 1998–2001 *Reissue based on LONG HORN model 4423 (see earlier listing), but with truss-rod at body end, various finishes.*

LONGHORN PRO 2000–01 *Similar to 58 LONGHORN (see earlier listing), but with metal key tuners and four-saddle bridge/tailpiece.*

LONGHORN 2006–07 *Similar to LONGHORN PRO (see earlier listing), but with two controls (volume, tone) and three-way selector.*

Other basses produced by Danelectro include:
U.S.
Long Horn model 4623 six-string 1958–69
Short Horn model 3412 1959–67
Short Horn six-string 1959–67
UB-2 six-string 1956–59

Korea
DC 1999–2001
Hodad 2000–01

EPIPHONE

U.S.

RIVOLI EBV-232 1960–70 *Semi-acoustic twin-cutaway body, one pickup.*
- Glued-in neck with rosewood fingerboard, dot markers; 30.5–inch scale, 20 frets; truss-rod adjuster at headstock end; two-a-side tuners with rear-facing plastic keys (horizontal metal type from c1960).
- Hollow twin-cutaway bound body with two f-holes; sunburst, natural or red.
- One plastic-cover (metal-cover from c1964) four-polepiece pickup.
- Two controls (volume, tone) and tone pushbutton switch, all on body; front-mounted jack socket.
- Black laminated plastic pickguard.
- Single-saddle bridge/tailpiece.

Other basses produced by Epiphone include:
U.S.
Embassy Deluxe 1963–70
Newport 1961–70

Japan
EA-260 semi-acoustic 1971–76
ET-285 1973–76
Scroll II 1977–79
Elite EB-3 2002–
Elite Thunderbird 2002–
Elitist EB-3 2003–
Elitist Thunderbird 2003–

Taiwan
Genesis 1979–80

Korea
Allen Woody Signature 2002–current
EB-3 five-string 2000–
EBM-4 1991–
Les Paul Standard five-string 2000–
Les Paul Special 2006–current
Nikki Sixx Blackbird Signature 2007–current

FENDER

This section is split into three levels. First, there is a division by place of manufacture (U.S., Mexico, Japan, and Korea, in that order). Within those divisions, there are headings for Jazz, Precision, and Other Models. Then, within the U.S., Mexico, and Japan Jazz and Precision listings, models are further split into what we have called Regular, Replica, and Revised models. For Squier By Fender models, see the later SQUIER section.

Features common to all Fender basses, unless stated otherwise:
- Bolt-on neck.
- Unbound fingerboard.
- 34–inch scale, 20 frets.
- Four in-line tuners with metal keys.
- Four-screw neckplate.
- Solid unbound body.
- Nickel- or chrome-plated hardware.

FENDER U.S.

U.S.-MADE JAZZ MODELS
U.S. Jazz basses are divided into three sections: U.S. Regular; U.S. Replica; U.S. Revised.

U.S. REGULAR JAZZ MODELS
Listed here in chronological order are what we regard as regular versions of the Jazz model.

JAZZ first version 1960–62 *Two dual-concentric controls.*
- Maple neck with rosewood fingerboard, dot markers; truss-rod adjuster at body end.
- Contoured double-cutaway offset-waist body; sunburst or colours.
- Two black eight-polepiece straight pickups.
- Two dual-concentric controls (each volume/tone) and jack socket, all on metal plate adjoining pickguard.
- White or tortoiseshell laminated plastic pickguard.
- Four-saddle bridge/tailpiece; body-mounted individual string-mutes.

JAZZ second version 1962–75 *Three controls.*
Similar to JAZZ first version (see earlier listing), except:
- Fretted bound maple neck (from c1969), or maple neck with rosewood fingerboard (bound from c1965, block markers (from c1966).
- Body sunburst, natural or colours.
- Three controls (two volume, one tone) and jack socket, all on metal plate adjoining pickguard.
- No body-mounted individual string-mutes.

JAZZ third version 1975–81 *'Bullet' truss-rod adjuster at headstock end, three-screw neckplate.*
Similar to JAZZ second version (see earlier listing), except:
- 'Bullet' truss-rod adjuster at headstock end; three-screw neckplate.
- White or black laminated plastic pickguard.
Also ANTIGUA JAZZ, with white/brown shaded body finish and matching colour laminated plastic pickguard (1977–79). Also INTERNATIONAL COLOUR JAZZ, with special colour body finishes, white laminated plastic pickguard and black-plated pickguard screws (1981).

STANDARD JAZZ first version 1981–83 *Truss-rod adjuster at body end, two white straight pickups.*
- Fretted maple neck, or maple neck with rosewood fingerboard, dot markers; truss-rod adjuster at body end.
- Contoured double-cutaway offset-waist body; sunburst, natural or colours.
- Two white eight-polepiece straight pickups.
- Three controls (two volume, one tone) and jack socket, all on metal plate adjoining pickguard.
- White laminated plastic pickguard.
- Four-saddle bridge/tailpiece.

STANDARD JAZZ second version 1983–85 *Controls and jack socket on pickguard.*
Similar to STANDARD JAZZ first version (see earlier listing), except:
- Truss-rod adjuster at headstock end.
- Controls and jack socket on pickguard.
- White plastic pickguard.

AMERICAN STANDARD JAZZ second version
1995–2000 *20 frets, through-body stringing.*
- Fretted maple neck (from 1997), or maple neck with rosewood fingerboard (fretless option from 1999), dot markers; truss-rod adjuster at body end.
- Contoured double-cutaway offset-waist body; sunburst, natural or colours.
- Two black eight-polepiece straight pickups.
- Three controls (two volume, one tone) and jack

socket, all on metal plate adjoining pickguard.
- White laminated plastic pickguard.
- Four-saddle bridge with through-body stringing.

AMERICAN JAZZ 2000–07 *20 frets, through-body stringing, cream laminated plastic pickguard.*
Similar to AMERICAN STANDARD JAZZ second version (see earlier listing), except:
- Fretted maple neck, or maple neck with rosewood fingerboard (fretless option from 2004).
- Volume with push-switch (from 2003).
- Cream laminated plastic pickguard (also black or black laminated plastic from 2003).

AMERICAN STANDARD JAZZ third version
2008–current *20 frets, through-body stringing, heavier-duty bridge.*
Similar to AMERICAN JAZZ (see earlier listing), except:
- White, cream or tortoiseshell laminated plastic pickguard.
- Heavier-duty four-saddle bridge with through-body stringing.

HIGHWAY ONE JAZZ first version 2003–06 *Satin finish body, truss-rod adjuster at headstock end.*
- Maple neck with rosewood fingerboard, dot markers; truss-rod adjuster at headstock end.
- Contoured double-cutaway offset-waist body; sunburst or colours, satin finish.
- Two black eight-polepiece straight pickups.
- Three controls (two volume, one tone) and jack socket, all on metal plate adjoining pickguard.
- White laminated plastic pickguard.
- Four-saddle bridge/tailpiece.

HIGHWAY ONE JAZZ second version 2006–current
Satin finish body, truss-rod adjuster at body end.
Similar to HIGHWAY ONE JAZZ first version (see earlier listing), except:
- Truss-rod adjuster at body end; '70s-style larger headstock logo
- Cream laminated plastic pickguard.
- Heavier-duty four-saddle bridge/tailpiece.

U.S. REPLICA JAZZ MODELS
Listed here in alphabetical/numerical order are the replica versions of various standard U.S. Jazz models (see earlier U.S. Regular Jazz models section).

AMERICAN VINTAGE '62 JAZZ 1998–current *Replica of 1960–62 period original (see JAZZ first version listing in earlier U.S. Regular Jazz models section).*

AMERICAN VINTAGE '75 JAZZ 1999–current *Replica of 1975-period original (see JAZZ third version listing in earlier U.S. Regular Jazz models section).*

'64 JAZZ 1999–current *Replica of 1964-period original (see JAZZ second version listing in earlier U.S. Regular Jazz models section). Available with three finish distress degrees: N.O.S., Closet Classic and Relic. Custom Shop production.*

RELIC 60s JAZZ 1996–98 *Distressed finish replica of 1960s-period original (see JAZZ second version in earlier U.S. Regular Jazz models section. Custom Shop production.*

'62 JAZZ 1982–98 *Replica of 1960–62 period original (see JAZZ first version listing in earlier U.S. Regular Jazz models section).*

'62 JAZZ LIMITED EDITION 1987–89 *Replica of 1960–62 period original (see JAZZ first version listing in earlier U.S. Regular Jazz models section) but with blond body finish and gold-plated hardware.*

U.S. REVISED JAZZ MODELS
Listed here in alphabetical/numerical order are what we regard as revised and adapted versions of the Jazz model.

AMERICAN CLASSIC JAZZ 1995–96 *Revised-shape smaller body, two four-polepiece straight pickups, four controls, block markers.*
- Fretted bound maple neck, or maple neck with bound rosewood fingerboard, block markers; 34–inch scale, 22 frets; truss-rod adjuster at body end; smaller headstock.
- Revised-shape contoured double-cutaway offset-waist smaller body; sunburst or natural.
- Two black four-polepiece straight pickups.
- Three controls (volume, middle, balance) and one dual-concentric control (treble/bass), all on metal plate adjoining pickguard; side-mounted jack socket; active circuit.
- White pearl or tortoiseshell laminated plastic pickguard.

139

- Four-saddle bridge/tailpiece with optional through-body stringing.

Also AMERICAN CLASSIC JAZZ FMT, with figured maple top body (1995–96).
Custom Shop production.

AMERICAN CLASSIC JAZZ FMT *See earlier AMERICAN CLASSIC JAZZ listing.*

AMERICAN CLASSIC JAZZ V FMT 1995–96 *Five strings, revised-shape smaller body with figured top, four controls, block markers.*
Similar to AMERICAN CLASSIC JAZZ (see earlier listing), except:
- Five in-line tuners with metal keys.
- Body with figured maple top.
- Two black five-polepiece straight pickups.
- Five-saddle bridge/tailpiece with optional through-body stringing.

AMERICAN DELUXE JAZZ 1998–current *Revised-shape smaller body, four controls.*
- Fretted maple neck, or maple neck with rosewood fingerboard (fretless option), dot markers; 34–inch scale, 22 frets; truss-rod adjuster at body end.
- Revised-shape contoured double-cutaway offset-waist smaller body; sunburst, natural or colours.
- Two black four-polepiece (eight-polepiece from 1999) straight pickups.
- Three controls (volume, middle, balance) and one dual-concentric control (treble/bass), all on metal plate next to pickguard; side-mounted jack socket; active circuit.
- White or tortoiseshell laminated plastic pickguard (also gold or white pearl laminated plastic from 2004).
- Four-saddle bridge/tailpiece with optional through-body stringing.

Also AMERICAN DELUXE JAZZ ASH, with ash body; sunburst or colours (2004–current).

AMERICAN DELUXE JAZZ ASH *See earlier AMERICAN DELUXE JAZZ listing.*

AMERICAN DELUXE JAZZ V 1998–current *Five strings, revised-shape smaller body, four controls.*
Similar to AMERICAN DELUXE JAZZ (see earlier listing), except:
- Fretted maple neck, or maple neck with pau ferro fingerboard; five in-line tuners with metal keys (four-plus-one tuners from 2003).

- Two black five-polepiece (ten-polepiece from 1999) straight pickups.
- Five-saddle bridge/tailpiece with optional though-body stringing.

Also AMERICAN DELUXE JAZZ V ASH, with ash body; sunburst or colours (2004–current).

AMERICAN DELUXE JAZZ V ASH *See earlier AMERICAN DELUXE JAZZ V listing.*

AMERICAN DELUXE JAZZ FMT or **QMT** 2001–06
Revised-shape smaller body with figured top, four controls on body, gold-plated hardware.
- Fretted bound maple neck, or maple neck with bound rosewood fingerboard, block markers; 34–inch scale, 21 frets; truss-rod adjuster at body end.
- Revised-shape contoured double-cutaway offset-waist smaller body with figured maple top; sunburst, natural or colours.
- Two black eight-polepiece straight pickups.
- Three controls (volume, middle, balance) and one dual-concentric control (treble/bass), all on body; side-mounted jack socket; active circuit.
- No pickguard.
- Four-saddle bridge/tailpiece with optional through-body stringing.
- Gold-plated hardware.

AMERICAN DELUXE JAZZ V FMT or **QMT** 2002–06
Five strings, revised-shape smaller body with figured top, four controls on body, gold-plated hardware.
Similar to AMERICAN DELUXE JAZZ FMT (see earlier listing), except:
- Maple neck with bound pau ferro fingerboard only; four-plus-one tuners with metal keys.
- Two black logo ten-polepiece straight pickups.
- Five-saddle bridge/tailpiece with optional through-body stringing.

AMERICAN JAZZ V 2000–07 *Five strings, 20 frets, through-body stringing, one straight string-guide.*
Similar to AMERICAN JAZZ (see listing in earlier U.S. Regular Jazz models section), except:
- Maple neck with pau ferro fingerboard only; five in-line tuners with metal keys (four-plus-one tuners from 2007).
- Two black ten-polepiece straight pickups.
- Five-saddle bridge/tailpiece with though-body stringing.

AMERICAN STANDARD JAZZ first version 1988–94
Revised-shape body with elongated left horn, 22 frets.
- Maple neck with rosewood fingerboard, dot markers; 34–inch scale, 22 frets; truss-rod adjuster at headstock end.
- Revised-shape contoured double-cutaway offset-waist body with elongated left horn; sunburst or colours.
- Two black eight-polepiece straight pickups.
- Three controls (two volume, one tone) and jack socket, all on metal plate adjoining pickguard.
- White or black laminated plastic pickguard.
- Four-saddle bridge/tailpiece.

AMERICAN STANDARD JAZZ V first version
1995–2000 *Five strings, 20 frets, through-body stringing, two round string guides.*
Similar to AMERICAN STANDARD JAZZ second version (see listing in earlier U.S. Regular Jazz models section), except:
- Maple neck with pau ferro fingerboard only; five in-line tuners with metal keys.
- Two black ten-polepiece straight pickups.
- Five-saddle bridge with through-body stringing.

AMERICAN STANDARD JAZZ V second version
2008–current *Five strings, 20 frets, through-body stringing, heavier-duty bridge.*
Similar to AMERICAN STANDARD JAZZ third version (see listing in earlier US Regular Jazz models section), except:
- Four-plus-one tuners with metal keys.
- Two black ten-polepiece straight pickups.
- Heavier-duty 5-saddle bridge with thru-body stringing.

ANTIGUA JAZZ *See JAZZ third version in earlier U.S. Regular Jazz models section.*

CUSTOM CLASSIC JAZZ 2001–current *Revised-shape body, block markers.*
- Fretted maple neck, or maple neck with rosewood fingerboard, block markers; 34–inch scale, 21 frets; truss-rod adjuster body end.
- Revised-shape contoured double-cutaway offset-waist body; sunburst or colours.
- Two black eight-polepiece straight pickups.
- Three controls (volume, middle, balance) and one dual-concentric control (treble/bass), all on metal plate adjoining pickguard; side-mounted jack socket; active circuit.

- White pearl or tortoiseshell laminated plastic pickguard.
- Four-saddle bridge/tailpiece with optional through-body stringing.
Custom Shop production.

CUSTOM CLASSIC JAZZ V 2001–current *Five strings, revised-shape body, block markers, four-plus-one tuners.*
Similar to CUSTOM CLASSIC JAZZ (see earlier listing), except:
- Fretted maple neck, or maple neck with pau ferro fingerboard; four-plus-one tuners with metal keys.
- Two black ten-polepiece straight pickups.
- Five-saddle bridge/tailpiece with optional through-body stringing.
Custom Shop production.

DELUXE JAZZ 1995–97 *Revised-shape smaller body, two four-polepiece straight pickups, four controls, smaller headstock.*
- Fretted maple neck, or maple neck with rosewood fingerboard (fretless option from 1997), dot markers; 34–inch scale, 22 frets; truss-rod adjuster at body end; smaller headstock.
- Revised-shape contoured double-cutaway offset-waist smaller body; sunburst or colours.
- Two black four-polepiece straight pickups.
- Three controls (volume, middle, balance) and one dual-concentric control (treble/bass), all on metal plate adjoining pickguard; side-mounted jack socket; active circuit.
- White pearl or tortoiseshell laminated plastic pickguard.
- Four-saddle bridge/tailpiece with optional through-body stringing.

DELUXE JAZZ V 1995–97 *Five strings, revised-shape smaller body, two four-polepiece straight pickups, four controls, smaller headstock.*
Similar to DELUXE JAZZ (see earlier listing), except:
- Maple neck with rosewood fingerboard only; five in-line tuners with metal keys.
- Two black five-polepiece straight pickups.
- Five-saddle bridge/tailpiece with optional though-body stringing.

GOLD/GOLD JAZZ 1981–83 *Gold body, two white straight pickups, gold-plated hardware.*
Similar to STANDARD JAZZ first version (see listing in

earlier U.S. Regular Jazz models section), except:

- Fretted bound maple neck only.
- Body gold only.
- Heavier-duty four-saddle bridge/tailpiece.
- Gold-plated hardware.

INTERNATIONAL COLOUR JAZZ *See JAZZ third version in earlier U.S. Regular Jazz models section.*

JACO PASTORIUS JAZZ 1999–current *No pickguard, three controls and jack socket on metal plate.*
Similar to JAZZ second version (see listing in earlier U.S. Regular Jazz models section), except:

- Maple neck with rosewood fingerboard (fretless option, pau ferro from 2001; fretless only from 2003), dot markers; truss-rod adjuster at body end.
- Contoured double-cutaway offset-waist body; sunburst only.
- Two black eight-polepiece straight pickups.
- Three controls (two volume, one tone) and jack socket, all on metal plate..
- No pickguard.
- Four-saddle bridge/tailpiece.

JACO PASTORIUS TRIBUTE JAZZ 1999–current *No pickguard, three controls and jack socket on metal plate, row of screw holes in front of bridge/tailpiece.*
Similar to JACO PASTORIUS JAZZ (see earlier listing), except:

- Maple neck with fretless rosewood fingerboard only.
- Body distressed sunburst only.
- Row of four screw holes in front of bridge/tailpiece.
Custom Shop production.

JAZZ PLUS 1990–94 *Revised-shape smaller body, controls on body, no pickguard.*

- Fretted maple neck, or maple neck with rosewood fingerboard, dot markers; 34–inch scale, 22 frets; truss-rod adjuster at headstock end; smaller headstock.
- Revised-shape contoured double-cutaway offset-waist smaller body; sunburst, natural or colours.
- Two black plain straight pickups.
- Two dual-concentric controls (volume/balance, treble/bass) and rotary selector, all on body; side-mounted jack socket; active circuit.
- No pickguard.
- Four-saddle bridge/tailpiece.

JAZZ PLUS V 1990–94 *Five strings, revised-shape smaller body, controls on body, no pickguard.*
Similar to JAZZ PLUS (see earlier listing), except:

- Maple neck with rosewood fingerboard only; five in-line tuners with metal keys.
- Five-saddle bridge/tailpiece.

MARCUS MILLER JAZZ V 2003–current *Five strings, signature on headstock.*

- Fretted bound maple neck, block markers; truss-rod adjuster at body end; four-plus-one tuners with metal keys; Marcus Miller signature on headstock.
- Body sunburst, natural or colours.
- Two black ten-polepiece straight pickups.
- Four controls (two volume, two tone), mini-switch and jack socket, all on pickguard.
- Revised-shape black laminated plastic pickguard.
- Five-saddle bridge/tailpiece with optional through-body stringing.

REGGIE HAMILTON JAZZ 2002–current *Revised-shape body, block markers, 21 frets, push-switch.*

- Maple neck with rosewood fingerboard, block markers; 34–inch scale, 21 frets; truss-rod adjuster at body end; five-screw neckplate; drop tuner on E-string.
- Revised-shape contoured double-cutaway offset-waist body; sunburst, black or red.
- One black eight-polepiece split pickup and one black eight-polepiece straight pickup.
- Three controls (volume, middle, balance), one dual-concentric control (treble/bass) and push-switch, all on metal plate adjoining pickguard; side-mounted jack socket; active circuit.
- White pearl, black pearl or tortoiseshell laminated plastic pickguard.
- Four-saddle bridge/tailpiece.
Custom Shop production.

REGGIE HAMILTON JAZZ V 2002–current *Five strings, revised-shape body, block markers, 21 frets, push-switch.*
Similar to REGGIE HAMILTON JAZZ (see earlier listing), except:

- Maple neck with pau ferro fingerboard; four-plus-one tuners with metal keys; drop tuner on B-string.
- One black ten-polepiece split pickup and one black ten-polepiece straight pickup.
- Five-saddle bridge/tailpiece with optional through-body stringing.
Custom Shop production.

VICTOR BAILEY JAZZ 2001–current *Signature on koa-face headstock.*

- Maple neck with rosewood fingerboard (fretless option from 2005), dot markers; 34–inch scale, 22 frets; truss-rod adjuster at body end; Victor Bailey signature on koa-face headstock,
- Revised-shape contoured double-cutaway offset-waist smaller body with koa top; natural only.
- Two black eight-polepiece straight pickups.
- Three controls (volume, middle, balance) and one dual-concentric control (treble/bass), all on body; side-mounted jack socket; active circuit.
- No pickguard.
- Four-saddle bridge/tailpiece with optional through-body stringing.
- Gold-plated hardware.

VICTOR BAILEY JAZZ V 2006–current *Five strings, signature on koa-face headstock.*
Similar to VICTOR BAILEY JAZZ (see earlier listing), except:
- Four-plus-one tuners with metal keys.
- Two black ten-polepiece straight pickups.
- Five-saddle bridge/tailpiece with optional through-body stringing.

50th ANNIVERSARY JAZZ 1996 *Commemorative neckplate.*
Similar to AMERICAN STANDARD JAZZ second version (see listing in earlier U.S. Regular Jazz models section), except:
- Maple neck with rosewood fingerboard only; commemorative neckplate.
- Body sunburst only.
- Gold-plated hardware.

50th ANNIVERSARY JAZZ V 1996 *Five strings, commemorative neckplate.*
Similar to 50TH ANNIVERSARY JAZZ (see earlier listing), except:
- Maple neck with pau ferro fingerboard only; five in-line tuners with metal keys.
- Two black ten-polepiece straight pickups.
- Five-saddle bridge with through-body stringing.

60th ANNIVERSARY JAZZ 2006 *Jewel emblem on headstock, commemorative neckplate.*
Similar to AMERICAN JAZZ (see listing in earlier U.S. Regular Jazz models section), except:

- Jewel emblem on headstock; commemorative neckplate.
- Body sunburst only.

U.S.-MADE PRECISION MODELS
U.S. Precision basses are divided into three sections: U.S. Regular; U.S. Replica and U.S. Revised.

U.S. REGULAR PRECISION MODELS
Listed here in chronological order are what we regard as regular versions of the Precision model.

PRECISION first version 1951–57 *Telecaster-style headstock, body-mounted pickup, controls on metal plate adjoining pickguard.*
- Fretted maple neck, dot markers; truss-rod adjuster at body end; enlarged Telecaster-style headstock.
- Slab double-cutaway body (contoured from c1954); blond only (or sunburst from c1954, or colours from c1956).
- One black four-polepiece small pickup.
- Two controls (volume, tone) on metal plate adjoining pickguard; side-mounted jack socket.
- Black pickguard (or white plastic from c1954).
- Two-saddle bridge with through-body stringing.

PRECISION second version 1957–81 *Enlarged Stratocaster-style headstock, controls on pickguard.*
- Fretted maple neck (1957–59, 1969–81), or maple neck with rosewood fingerboard (from c1959; maple fingerboard option 1967–69; fretless rosewood or maple option from c1970), dot markers; truss-rod adjuster at body end; enlarged Stratocaster-style headstock.
- Contoured double-cutaway body; sunburst, natural or colours.
- One black eight-polepiece split pickup.
- Two controls (volume, tone) and jack socket, all on pickguard.
- Gold anodised metal pickguard (white or tortoiseshell laminated plastic from c1959; black laminated plastic from c1975).
- Four-saddle bridge/tailpiece.

Also slab body version, with black or tortoiseshell laminated plastic pickguard (1966–67).
Also ANTIGUA PRECISION, with white/brown shaded body finish and matching colour laminated plastic pickguard (1977–79).
Also INTERNATIONAL COLOUR PRECISION, with special

143

colour body finishes, white laminated plastic pickguard and black-plated pickguard screws (1981).

STANDARD PRECISION first version 1981–83 *White split pickup.*
Similar to PRECISION second version (see earlier listing), except:
- Fretted maple neck, or maple neck with rosewood fingerboard, dot markers; truss-rod adjuster at body end.
- Contoured double-cutaway body; sunburst, natural or colours.
- One white eight-polepiece split pickup.
- Two controls (vol, tone) and jack socket, on pickguard.
- White laminated plastic pickguard.
- Four-saddle bridge/tailpiece.

STANDARD PRECISION second version 1983–85
White split pickup, truss-rod adjuster at headstock end.
Similar to STANDARD PRECISION first version (see earlier listing), except:
- Truss-rod adjuster at headstock end.
- White plastic pickguard.

AMERICAN STANDARD PRECISION first version
1995–2000 *Through-body stringing.*
- Fretted maple neck (from 1997), or maple neck with rosewood fingerboard (fretless option), dot markers; truss-rod adjuster at body end.
- Contoured double-cutaway body; sunburst, natural or colours.
- One black eight-polepiece split pickup.
- Two controls (volume, tone) and jack socket, all on pickguard.
- White laminated plastic pickguard.
- Four-saddle bridge with through-body stringing.

AMERICAN PRECISION 2000–07 *Through-body stringing, cream laminated plastic pickguard.*
Similar to AMERICAN STANDARD PRECISION (see earlier listing), except:
- Fretted maple neck, or maple neck with rosewood fingerboard.
- Volume with push-switch (from 2003).
- Cream laminated plastic pickguard (also black or black laminated plastic from 2003).

AMERICAN STANDARD PRECISION second version
2008–current *Through-body stringing, heavier-duty bridge.*

Similar to AMERICAN PRECISION (see earlier listing), except:
- White, cream or tortoiseshell laminated plastic pickguard.
- Heavier-duty four-saddle bridge with through-body stringing.

HIGHWAY ONE PRECISION first version 2003–06
Satin finish body, truss-rod adjuster at headstock end.
- Maple neck with rosewood fingerboard only, dot markers; truss-rod adjuster at headstock end.
- Contoured double-cutaway body; sunburst or colours, satin finish.
- One black eight-polepiece split pickup.
- Two controls (volume, tone) and jack socket, all on pickguard.
- White laminated plastic pickguard.
- Four-saddle bridge/tailpiece.

HIGHWAY ONE PRECISION second version
2006–current *Satin finish body, truss-rod adjuster at body end.*
Similar to HIGHWAY ONE PRECISION first version (see earlier listing), except:
- Truss-rod adjuster at body end; '70s-style larger headstock logo
- Cream laminated plastic pickguard.
- Heavier-duty four-saddle bridge/tailpiece.

U.S. REPLICA PRECISION MODELS
Listed here in alphabetical/numerical order are the replica versions of various standard U.S. Precision models (see earlier U.S. Regular Precision models section)..

AMERICAN VINTAGE '57 PRECISION 1998–current
Replica of 1957-period original (see PRECISION second version listing in earlier U.S. Regular Precision models section).

AMERICAN VINTAGE '62 PRECISION 1998–current
Replica of 1962-period original (see PRECISION second version listing in earlier U.S. Regular Precision models section).

'55 PRECISION 2003–06 *Replica of 1955-period original (see PRECISION first version listing in earlier U.S. Regular Precision models section). Available with three finish distress degrees: N.O.S., Closet Classic and Relic. Custom Shop production.*

'57 PRECISION 1982–98 *Replica of 1957-period original (see PRECISION second version listing in earlier U.S. Regular Precision models section).*

'57 PRECISION LIMITED EDITION 1987–89 *Replica of 1957-period original (see PRECISION second version listing in earlier U.S. Regular Precision models section) but with blond body finish and gold-plated hardware.*

'59 PRECISION 2000–current *Replica of 1959-period original (see PRECISION second version listing in earlier U.S. Regular Precision models section). Available with three finish distress degrees: N.O.S., Closet Classic and Relic. Custom Shop production.*

'62 PRECISION 1982–98 *Replica of 1962-period original (see PRECISION second version listing in earlier U.S. Regular Precision models section).*

'62 PRECISION LIMITED EDITION 1987–89 *Replica of 1962-period original (see PRECISION second version listing in earlier U.S. Regular Precision models section) but with blond body finish and gold-plated hardware.*

U.S. REVISED PRECISION MODELS

Listed here in alphabetical/numerical order are what we regard as revised and adapted versions of the Precision model.

AMERICAN DELUXE PRECISION 1998–current
Revised-shape smaller body, eight-polepiece split pickup and 16–polepiece pickup, four controls on pickguard.

- Fretted maple neck, or maple neck with rosewood fingerboard, dot markers; 34–inch scale, 22 frets; truss-rod adjuster at body end.
- Revised-shape contoured double-cutaway smaller body; sunburst, natural or colours.
- One black eight-polepiece split pickup and one black 16–polepiece pickup.
- Three controls (volume, middle, balance) and one dual-concentric control (treble/bass), all on pickguard; side-mounted jack socket; active circuit.
- White or black laminated plastic pickguard (also gold or white pearl laminated plastic from 2004, black pearl from 2005).
- Four-saddle bridge/tailpiece with optional through-body stringing.

Also AMERICAN DELUXE PRECISION ASH, with ash body; sunburst or colours (2004–06).

AMERICAN DELUXE PRECISION ASH *See earlier AMERICAN DELUXE PRECISION listing.*

AMERICAN DELUXE PRECISION V 1999–2006 *Five strings, revised-shape smaller body, ten-polepiece split pickup and 12–polepiece pickup, four controls on pickguard.*
Similar to AMERICAN DELUXE PRECISION (see earlier listing), except:

- Fretted maple neck, or maple neck with pau ferro fingerboard; five in-line tuners with metal keys.
- One black ten-polepiece split pickup and one black 12–polepiece pickup.
- Five-saddle bridge/tailpiece with optional though-body stringing.

Also AMERICAN DELUXE PRECISION V ASH, with ash body; sunburst or colours (2004–06).

AMERICAN DELUXE PRECISION V ASH *See earlier AMERICAN DELUXE PRECISION V listing.*

AMERICAN STANDARD PRECISION V 2008–current
Five strings, four-plus-one tuners.
Similar to AMERICAN STANDARD PRECISION second version (see listing in earlier US Regular Precision models section), except:

- Four-plus-one tuners with metal keys.
- One black ten-polepiece split pickup.
- Heavier-duty five-saddle bridge with through-body stringing.

ANTIGUA PRECISION *See PRECISION second version in earlier U.S. Regular Precision models section.*

CALIFORNIA PRECISION BASS SPECIAL 1997–98
California Series on headstock, Jazz-style neck.

- Jazz-style fretted maple neck, or maple neck with rosewood fingerboard, dot markers; truss-rod adjuster at headstock end; California series on headstock.
- Contoured double-cutaway body; sunburst or colours.
- One black eight-polepiece split pickup and one black eight-polepiece straight pickup.
- Three controls (two volume, one tone) on pickguard; side-mounted jack socket.
- Gold anodised metal pickguard.
- Four-saddle bridge/tailpiece.

DELUXE PRECISION 1995–98 *Revised-shape smaller body, eight-polepiece split pickup and 16–polepiece*

pickup, four controls on pickguard, smaller headstock.
- Fretted maple neck, or maple neck with rosewood fingerboard, dot markers; 34–inch scale, 22 frets; truss-rod adjuster at body end; smaller headstock.
- Revised-shape contoured double-cutaway smaller body; sunburst or colours.
- One black eight-polepiece split pickup and one black 16–polepiece pickup.
- Three controls (volume, middle, balance) and one dual-concentric control (treble/bass), all on pickguard; side-mounted jack socket; active circuit.
- White pearl or tortoiseshell laminated plastic pickguard.
- Four-saddle bridge/tailpiece with optional through-body stringing.

ELITE PRECISION 1983–85 *White plain split pickup.*
- Fretted maple neck, or maple neck with rosewood fingerboard (fretless option), dot markers; truss-rod adjuster at headstock end.
- Contoured double-cutaway body; sunburst, natural or colours.
- One white plain split pickup.
- Two controls (volume, tone) on pickguard; side-mounted jack socket; active circuit.
- White laminated plastic pickguard.
- Four-saddle bridge/tailpiece with individual fine-tuners.
Also GOLD ELITE PRECISION, with gold-plated hardware.

ELITE II PRECISION 1983–85 *Two white plain split pickups.*
Similar to ELITE PRECISION (see earlier listing), except:
- Two white plain split pickups.
- Three controls (two volume, one tone) and two mini-switches, all on pickguard.
Also GOLD ELITE II PRECISION, with gold-plated hardware.

GOLD ELITE PRECISION See earlier ELITE PRECISION listing.

GOLD ELITE II PRECISION See earlier ELITE II PRECISION listing.

HOT ROD PRECISION 1999–2000 *Black split pickup and black straight pickup, three controls on pickguard.*
- Fretted maple neck, or maple neck with rosewood fingerboard, dot markers; truss-rod adjuster at body end.

- Contoured double-cutaway body; sunburst, natural or colours.
- One black eight-polepiece split pickup and one black eight-polepiece straight pickup.
- Three controls (two volume, one tone) on pickguard; side-mounted jack socket.
- Tortoiseshell laminated plastic pickguard.
- Four-saddle bridge/tailpiece with optional through-body stringing.

INTERNATIONAL COLOUR PRECISION *See PRECISION second version in earlier Regular Precision models section.*

PINO PALLADINO PRECISION 2006–current *Signature on back of headstock.*
- Maple neck with rosewood fingerboard, dot markers; truss-rod adjuster at body end; Pino Palladino signature on back of headstock.
- Contoured double-cutaway body; red only, distressed finish.
- One black eight-polepiece split pickup.
- Two controls (volume, tone) and jack socket, all on pickguard.
- Tortoiseshell laminated plastic pickguard.
- Four-saddle bridge/tailpiece.
Custom Shop production.

PRECISION PLUS 1989–92 *Revised-shape body with elongated left horn, three-way selector and pushbutton-switch.*
- Fretted maple neck, or maple neck with rosewood fingerboard, dot markers; 34–inch scale, 22 frets; truss-rod adjuster at headstock end.
- Revised-shape contoured double-cutaway body with elongated left horn; sunburst, natural or colours.
- One black plain split pickup and one black plain straight pickup.
- Two controls (volume, tone), three-way selector, pushbutton-switch and jack socket, all on pickguard.
- White or cream laminated plastic pickguard.
- Four-saddle bridge/tailpiece with individual fine-tuners.

PRECISION PLUS DELUXE 1991–94 *Revised-shape smaller body, two dual-concentric controls on body, no pickguard.*
- Fretted maple neck, or maple neck with rosewood fingerboard, dot markers; 34–inch scale, 22 frets; truss-rod adjuster at headstock end; smaller headstock.

- Revised-shape contoured double-cutaway smaller body; sunburst, natural or colours.
- One black plain split pickup and one black plain straight pickup.
- Two dual-concentric controls (volume/balance, treble/bass) on body; side-mounted jack socket; active circuit.
- No pickguard.
- Four-saddle bridge/tailpiece with individual fine tuners.

PRECISION SPECIAL 1980–83 *Model name on headstock, white split pickup, three controls and mini-switch.*

- Fretted maple neck, or maple neck with rosewood fingerboard, dot markers; truss-rod adjuster at body end.
- Contoured double-cutaway body; blue, red or white.
- One white eight-polepiece split pickup.
- Three controls (volume, two tone), mini-switch and jack socket, all on pickguard; active circuit.
- White laminated plastic pickguard.
- Four-saddle bridge/tailpiece.
- Gold-plated hardware.

ROCCO PRESTIA PRECISION 1999 *Reversed split pickup, three controls on pickguard.*

- Fretted maple neck, dot markers; truss-rod adjuster at body end.
- Contoured double-cutaway body; natural, black or red.
- One black eight-polepiece reversed split pickup.
- Three controls (volume, two tone) on pickguard; side-mounted jack socket; active circuit.
- Black laminated plastic pickguard.
- Four-saddle bridge/tailpiece with optional through-body stringing.

TONY FRANKLIN FRETLESS PRECISION

2006–current *Tony Franklin signature on neckplate, fretless ebony fingerboard, three-way switch on pickguard.*

- Maple neck with fretless ebony fingerboard; truss-rod adjuster at body end; drop tuner on E-string; Tony Franklin signature on neckplate.
- Contoured double-cutaway body; sunburst or black.
- One black eight-polepiece split pickup and one black eight-polepiece straight pickup.
- Two controls (volume, tone), three-way switch and jack socket, all on pickguard.

- Tortoiseshell laminated plastic pickguard.
- Four-saddle bridge/tailpiece.

TONY FRANKLIN FRETTED PRECISION 2007–current
Tony Franklin signature on neckplate, three-way switch on pickguard.
Similar to TONE FRANKLIN FRETLESS PRECISION (see earlier listing), except:

- Fretted maple neck; no drop tuner on E-string.
- Body white or gold.
- Black laminated plastic pickguard.

VINTAGE PRECISION CUSTOM 1992–2000 *Enlarged Telecaster-style headstock, black split pickup and black straight pickup, two controls on metal plate adjoining pickguard.*

- Fretted maple neck, dot markers; truss-rod adjuster at body end; enlarged Telecaster-style headstock.
- Contoured double-cutaway body; sunburst or blond.
- One black eight-polepiece split pickup and one black eight-polepiece straight pickup.
- Two controls (volume, tone) on metal plate adjoining pickguard; side-mounted jack socket.
- White or black plastic pickguard.
- Two-saddle bridge with through-body stringing.

Custom Shop production.

WALNUT ELITE II PRECISION 1983–85 *Two white plain split pickups, walnut neck and body.*
Similar to ELITE II PRECISION (see earlier listing), except:

- Walnut neck with ebony fingerboard only (fretless option).
- Walnut body; natural only.
- Gold-plated hardware.

WALNUT PRECISION SPECIAL 1980–83 *Fretted walnut neck and body.*
Similar to PRECISION SPECIAL (see earlier listing), except:

- Fretted walnut neck only.
- Body natural only.
- One black eight-polepiece split pickup.
- Black laminated plastic pickguard.

50th ANNIVERSARY PRECISION 1996
Commemorative neckplate.
Similar to AMERICAN STANDARD PRECISION (see listing in earlier U.S. Regular Precision models section), except:

- Maple neck with rosewood fingerboard only; commemorative neckplate.
- Body sunburst only.
- Gold-plated hardware.

50th ANNIVERSARY AMERICAN PRECISION 2001
Commemorative neckplate.
Similar to AMERICAN PRECISION (see listing in earlier U.S. Regular Precision models section), except:
- Fretted maple neck only; commemorative neckplate.
- Body blonde only.
- Black plastic pickguard.

60th ANNIVERSARY PRECISION 2006 *Jewel emblem on headstock, commemorative neckplate.*
Similar to AMERICAN PRECISION (see listing in earlier U.S. Regular Precision models section), except:
- Jewel emblem on headstock; commemorative neckplate.
- Body sunburst only.

U.S.-MADE OTHER MODELS
Selected other U.S. Fender basses are listed here in alphabetical order of model name.

BASS VI *See later VI listing.*

MUSTANG 1966–81 *Model name on headstock, one small split pickup, two controls on metal plate adjoining pickguard.*
- Maple neck with rosewood fingerboard (fretted maple neck option from c1975), dot markers; 30–inch scale, 19 frets; truss-rod adjuster at body end.
- Contoured double-cutaway offset-waist small body; sunburst, natural or colours.
- One black plain small split pickup.
- Two controls (volume, tone) and jack socket, all on metal plate adjoining pickguard.
- White or white pearl or tortoiseshell laminated plastic pickguard (black laminated plastic from c1975).
- Four-saddle bridge with through-body stringing; individual string-mutes (1966–79).
Also ANTIGUA MUSTANG, with white/brown shaded body finish and matching colour laminated plastic pickguard (1977–79).
Also COMPETITION MUSTANG, with contrasting colour stripes on body (1968–73).

TELECASTER first version 1968–72 *Model name on enlarged Telecaster-style headstock, controls on metal plate adjoining pickguard.*
- Maple neck with maple fingerboard, or fretted maple neck (fretless option from c1970)
- Slab double-cutaway body; various colours.
- One four-polepiece small pickup.
- Two controls (volume, tone) on metal plate adjoining pickguard; side-mounted jack socket.
- White or white laminated plastic pickguard.
- Two-saddle bridge with through-body stringing.
Also BLUE FLOWER TELECASTER, with blue floral-pattern body finish and clear plastic pickguard (1968–72).
Also PAISLEY RED TELECASTER, with red paisley-pattern body finish and clear plastic pickguard (1968–72).

TELECASTER second version 1972–78 *Model name on enlarged Telecaster-style headstock, controls on pickguard.*
Similar to TELECASTER first version (see earlier listing), except:
- Fretted maple neck only; 'bullet' truss-rod adjuster at headstock end; three-screw neckplate.
- Body sunburst, natural or colours.
- One metal-cover split-polepiece pickup.
- Two controls (volume, tone) on pickguard.
- White or black laminated plastic pickguard.

VI 1961–75 *Six strings, model name on headstock.*
- Maple neck with rosewood fingerboard (bound from c1965), dot markers (blocks from c1966); 30–inch scale, 21 frets; truss-rod adjuster at body end; six in-line tuners with metal keys.
- Contoured offset-waist body; sunburst or colours.
- Three white six-polepiece pickups (each with flat metal surround 1961–63; each with 'saw-tooth' metal sides from c1963).
- Two controls (volume, tone) and jack socket, all on lower metal plate adjoining pickguard; three slide-switches (four from c1963) on metal plate inset into pickguard.
- White or tortoiseshell laminated plastic pickguard.
- Six-saddle bridge, spring-loaded string-mute (from c1963), vibrato tailpiece.

FENDER MEXICO

Each bass has 'Made In Mexico' somewhere on the instrument.

MEXICO-MADE JAZZ MODELS

Mexican Jazz models are divided into three sections: Mexico Regular, Mexico Replica and Mexico Revised.

MEXICO REGULAR JAZZ MODELS

Listed here in alphabetical order are what we regard as Mexico-made regular versions of the Jazz model.

SPECIAL JAZZ *U.K. designation for STANDARD JAZZ (see later listing).*

SQUIER SERIES JAZZ 1994–96 *Small Squier Series logo on headstock.*
Similar to TRADITIONAL JAZZ (see later listing), except:
- Small Squier Series logo on headstock.
Replaced Korean-made version (see listing in later Korea Jazz models section).

STANDARD JAZZ 1991–current *Silver Fender headstock logo, controls and jack socket on metal plate adjoining white laminated plastic pickguard.*
- Maple neck with rosewood fingerboard (fretless option from 1997), dot markers; truss-rod adjuster at body end (at headstock end from 1996).
- Contoured double-cutaway offset-waist body; sunburst or colours.
- Two black eight-polepiece straight pickups.
- Three controls (two volume, one tone) and jack socket, all on metal plate adjoining pickguard.
- White laminated plastic pickguard.
- Four-saddle bridge/tailpiece.
Originally known as SPECIAL JAZZ in U.K.

TRADITIONAL JAZZ 1996–97 *Black Fender headstock logo, controls and jack socket on white plastic pickguard.*
- Maple neck with rosewood fingerboard, dot markers; truss-rod adjuster at headstock end.
- Contoured double-cutaway offset-waist body; black, red or white.
- Two black eight-polepiece straight pickups.
- Three controls (two volume, one tone) and jack socket, all on pickguard.
- White plastic pickguard.
- Four-saddle bridge/tailpiece.
Replaced SQUIER SERIES JAZZ (see earlier listing).

MEXICO REPLICA JAZZ MODELS

Listed here in alphabetical order are the Mexico-made replica versions of various standard U.S. Jazz models (see earlier U.S. Regular Jazz models section).

CLASSIC '60s JAZZ 2004–current *Replica of 1960s-period original (see JAZZ second version listing in earlier U.S. Regular Jazz models section).*

MEXICO REVISED JAZZ MODELS

Listed here in alphabetical order are what we regard as Mexico-made revised and adapted versions of the Jazz model.

DELUXE ACTIVE JAZZ 1997–current *Two four-polepiece straight pickups, four controls.*
except:
- Maple neck with rosewood fingerboard, dot markers; truss-rod adjuster at headstock end.
- Contoured double-cutaway offset-waist body; sunburst or colours.
- Two black four-polepiece straight pickups.
- Three controls (volume, middle, balance) and one dual-concentric control (treble/bass), all on metal plate adjoining pickguard; side-mounted jack socket; active circuit.
- Tortoiseshell laminated plastic pickguard.
- Four-saddle bridge/tailpiece.

DELUXE ACTIVE JAZZ V 1998–current *Five strings, two five-polepiece straight pickups, four controls.*
Similar to DELUXE ACTIVE JAZZ (see earlier listing), except:
- Maple neck with pau ferro fingerboard (from 1999).
- Five in-line tuners with metal keys.
- Two black five-polepiece straight pickups.
- Five-saddle bridge/tailpiece.

DELUXE POWER JAZZ 2006–current *Two eight-polepiece straight pickups, four controls.*
- Maple neck with rosewood fingerboard, dot markers; truss-rod adjuster at body end.
- Contoured double-cutaway offset-waist body; sunburst only.
- Two black eight-polepiece straight pickups and piezo pickup system in bridge.
- Three controls (two volume, one tone for magnetic pickups) and one dual-concentric control (volume/tone for piezo pickup), all on metal plate

adjoining pickguard; side-mounted jack socket; active circuit.

- Tortoiseshell laminated plastic pickguard.
- Four-saddle bridge/tailpiece with built-in piezo pickup system.

DUFF McKAGAN JAZZ SPECIAL 2007–current *Black-finished neck, skull-engraved neckplate.*

- Black-finished maple neck with rosewood fingerboard, dot markers; truss-rod adjuster at body end; black-face headstock; skull-engraved neckplate.
- Precision-style contoured double-cutaway body; white only.
- One black eight-polepiece split pickup and one black eight-polepiece straight pickup.
- Three controls (two volume, one tone) and three-way selector, all on body; side-mounted jack socket.
- No pickguard.
- Four-saddle bridge/tailpiece.
- Black-plated hardware.

Known officially as DUFF McKAGAN P-BASS, but Jazz Bass Special actually on headstock.

REGGIE HAMILTON STANDARD JAZZ 2005–current
Black split pickup and black straight pickup, four controls and mini-switch.

- Maple neck with rosewood fingerboard, dot markers; truss-rod adjuster at body end; drop-tuner on E-string.
- Contoured double-cutaway offset-waist body; sunburst or black.
- One black eight-polepiece split pickup and one black eight-polepiece straight pickup.
- Three controls (volume, middle, balance), one dual-concentric control (treble/bass) and mini-switch, all on metal plate adjoining pickguard; side-mounted jack socket; active circuit.
- Tortoiseshell or black laminated plastic pickguard.
- Four-saddle bridge/tailpiece.

STANDARD JAZZ V 1998–current *Five strings, two ten-polepiece straight pickups, three controls.*
Similar to STANDARD JAZZ (see listing in earlier Mexico Replica Jazz models section), except:

- Maple neck with pau ferro fingerboard.
- Five in-line tuners with metal keys.
- Two black ten-polepiece straight pickups.
- Five-saddle bridge/tailpiece.

MEXICO-MADE PRECISION MODELS
Mexican Precision models are divided into three sections: Mexico Regular, Mexico Replica and Mexico Revised.

MEXICO REGULAR PRECISION MODELS
Listed here in alphabetical order are what we regard as Mexico-made regular versions of the Precision model.

SPECIAL PRECISION *U.K. designation for STANDARD PRECISION (see later listing).*

SQUIER SERIES PRECISION 1994–96 *Small Squier Series logo on headstock.*
Similar to TRADITIONAL PRECISION (see later listing), except:

- Small Squier Series logo on headstock.
Replaced Korean-made version (see listing in later Korea Precision models section).

STANDARD PRECISION 1991–current *Silver Fender headstock logo, white laminated plastic pickguard.*

- Maple neck with rosewood fingerboard, dot markers; truss-rod adjuster at body end (at headstock end from 2003).
- Contoured double-cutaway body; sunburst or colours.
- One black eight-polepiece split pickup.
- Two controls (volume, tone) and jack socket, all on pickguard.
- White laminated plastic pickguard.
- Four-saddle bridge/tailpiece.
Originally known as SPECIAL PRECISION in UK.

TRADITIONAL PRECISION 1996–97 *Black Fender headstock logo, white plastic pickguard.*

- Maple neck with rosewood fingerboard, dot markers; truss-rod adjuster at headstock end.
- Contoured double-cutaway body; black, red or white.
- One black eight-polepiece split pickup.
- Two controls (volume, tone) and jack socket, all on pickguard.
- White plastic pickguard.
- Four-saddle bridge/tailpiece.
Replaced SQUIER SERIES PRECISION (see earlier listing).

MEXICO REPLICA PRECISION MODELS
Listed here in alphabetical order are the Mexico-made replica versions of various standard U.S. Precision models (see earlier U.S. Regular Precision models section).

CLASSIC '50s PRECISION 2005–current *Replica of 1950s-period original (see PRECISION second version listing in earlier U.S. Regular Precision models section).*

MEXICO REVISED PRECISION MODELS

Listed here in alphabetical/numerical order are what we regard as Mexico-made revised and adapted versions of the Precision model.

DELUXE BIG BLOCK PRECISION 2005–current *Block markers, no pickguard.*
- Maple neck with rosewood fingerboard, block markers; truss-rod adjuster at body end; black-face headstock.
- Contoured double-cutaway body; black only.
- One black 16–polepiece pickup.
- Two controls (volume, tone) and mini-switch, all on metal plate; side-mounted jack socket; active circuit.
- No pickguard.
- Four-saddle bridge; optional through-body stringing.

DELUXE ACTIVE PRECISION SPECIAL 2005–current *Black split pickup and black straight pickup, gold plastic pickguard.*
Similar to DELUXE PRECISION SPECIAL (see later listing), except:
- Body various colours.
- Three controls (volume, middle, balance) and one dual-concentric control (treble/bass), all on pickguard; side-mounted jack socket; active circuit.
- Gold plastic pickguard.
- Four-saddle bridge/tailpiece.

DELUXE PRECISION SPECIAL 1999–2004 *Black split pickup and black straight pickup, gold metal pickguard.*
- Jazz-style fretted maple neck, or maple neck with rosewood fingerboard, dot markers; truss-rod adjuster at headstock end.
- Contoured double-cutaway body; sunburst or colours.
- One black eight-polepiece split pickup and one black eight-polepiece straight pickup.
- Three controls (two volume, one tone) on pickguard; side-mounted jack socket.
- Gold anodised metal pickguard.
- Four-saddle bridge/tailpiece.

DUFF MCKAGAN P-BASS *See DUFF MCKAGAN JAZZ SPECIAL listing in earlier Mexico Revised Jazz models section.*

MARK HOPPUS PRECISION 2002–current *Name on neckplate, Jazz-style body.*
- Maple neck with rosewood fingerboard, dot markers; truss-rod adjuster at headstock end; Mark Hoppus on neckplate.
- Jazz-style contoured double-cutaway offset-waist body; blue, green or pink.
- One black eight-polepiece split pickup.
- One control (volume) and jack socket on pickguard.
- Jazz-style white pearl laminated plastic pickguard.
- Four-saddle bridge with through-body stringing.

MIKE DIRNT PRECISION 2004–current *One split pickup, two controls on metal plate.*
- Maple neck with rosewood fingerboard, dot markers; truss-rod adjuster at body end.
- Contoured double-cutaway body; sunburst, black or white.
- One black eight-polepiece split pickup.
- Two controls (volume, tone) on metal plate adjoining pickguard; side-mounted jack socket.
- White plastic pickguard.
- Four-saddle bridge/tailpiece.

P-BASS SPECIAL 1994–96 *Revised-shape body, Black split pickup and black straight pickup, two dual-concentric controls on body.*
- Maple neck with rosewood fingerboard, dot markers; 34–inch scale, 22 frets; truss-rod adjuster at headstock end.
- Revised-shape contoured double-cutaway smaller body; sunburst or colours.
- One black eight-polepiece split pickup and one black eight-polepiece straight pickup.
- Two dual-concentric controls (volume/balance, treble/bass) on body; side-mounted jack socket; active circuit.
- Black laminated plastic pickguard.
- Four-saddle bridge/tailpiece.

60th ANNIVERSARY STANDARD PRECISION 2006 *Commemorative neckplate.*
Similar to STANDARD PRECISION (see listing in Mexico Replica Precision models section), except:
- Commemorative neckplate.
- Body silver grey only.

FENDER JAPAN

This section lists only the models marketed outside of Japan, all of which have 'Made In Japan' or 'Crafted in Japan' somewhere on the instrument. It does not cover the basses produced solely for the Japanese market, which include interpretations of Fender's established designs in combinations of construction, components, and cosmetics.

The periods of availability for models sold in Japan often differ greatly to those of the same models officially sold in export markets. These export models, listed here, often appear to come and go, usually because demand from a particular distributor fluctuates. For that reason, certain Japanese models are irregularly removed from and then replaced in Fender's catalogues in the U.S.A. and Europe – while production of the model in Japan might well remain continuous. This interrupted availability is confusing from a Western point of view and makes it difficult to accurately pin down the true periods of production, so please bear that in mind when you consult the listings here.

JAPAN-MADE JAZZ MODELS

Japanese Jazz models are divided into three sections: Japan Regular, Japan Replica, and Japan Revised.

JAPAN REGULAR JAZZ MODELS

Listed here in alphabetical order are what we regard as Japan-made exported regular versions of the Jazz model.

STANDARD JAZZ 1988–91 *Modern-style 'thick' Fender headstock logo in silver.*
- Maple neck with rosewood fingerboard (fretless option available until 1997), dot markers; truss-rod adjuster at body end.
- Contoured double-cutaway offset-waist body; black or white.
- Two black eight-polepiece straight pickups.
- Three controls (two volume, one tone) and jack socket, all on metal plate adjoining pickguard.
- White laminated plastic pickguard.
- Four-saddle bridge/tailpiece.

Replaced by Mexican-made version in 1991 (see STANDARD JAZZ listing in earlier Mexico Replica Jazz models section).

JAPAN REPLICA JAZZ MODELS

Listed here in alphabetical/numerical order are the Japan-made exported replica versions of various standard U.S. Jazz models (see earlier U.S. Regular Jazz models section).

SQUIER VINTAGE SERIES '62 JAZZ 1982–83 *Replica of 1962-period U.S. original (see JAZZ second version listing in earlier U.S. Regular Jazz models section). Small Squier Series logo on headstock. Replaced by Squier-branded version from 1983 (see later Squier main entry).*

60s JAZZ 1989–94 *Replica of 1960s-period U.S. original (see JAZZ second version listing in earlier U.S. Regular Jazz models section).*

'75 JAZZ 1992–99 *Replica of 1970s-period U.S. original (see JAZZ third version listing in earlier U.S. Regular Jazz models section).*

JAPAN REVISED JAZZ MODELS

Listed here in alphabetical/numerical order are what we regard as Japan-made exported revised and adapted versions of the Jazz model.

AERODYNE JAZZ 2003–current *Model name on black-face headstock.*
- Maple neck with rosewood fingerboard, dot markers; truss-rod adjuster at body end.
- Contoured double-cutaway offset-waist bound body with curved top; black only.
- One black eight-polepiece split pickup and one black eight-polepiece straight pickup.
- Three controls (two volume, one tone) and jack socket (black-plated Strat-style from 2005), on body.
- No pickguard.
- Four-saddle bridge/tailpiece.

CONTEMPORARY JAZZ *See later JAZZ SPECIAL listing.*

CONTEMPORARY JAZZ SPECIAL *See later JAZZ SPECIAL listing.*

FOTO FLAME 60s JAZZ 1994–96 *Fake figured wood finish on neck and body.*
Similar to 60s JAZZ (see listing in earlier Japan Replica Jazz models section), except:
- Foto Flame fake figured wood finish neck.

- Foto Flame fake figured wood finish body; sunbursts or natural.
- White or white pearl laminated plastic pickguard.

GEDDY LEE JAZZ 1998–current *Fretted black bound maple neck, black block markers.*
Similar to '75 JAZZ (see listing in earlier Japan Replica Jazz models section), except:
- Fretted black bound maple neck only, black block markers.
- Body black only.
- Heavier-duty four-saddle bridge/tailpiece.

JAZZ SPECIAL 1985–91 *Model name on headstock.*
- Black-finished maple neck with rosewood fingerboard (fretless option), dot markers; truss-rod adjuster at body end; black-face headstock.
- Precision-style contoured double-cutaway body; various colours.
- One black eight-polepiece split pickup and one black eight-polepiece straight pickup.
- Three controls (two volume, one tone) and three-way selector, all on body; side-mounted jack socket.
- No pickguard.
- Four-saddle bridge/tailpiece.
- Black-plated hardware.
Originally known as P-J model (1985).
Also known as CONTEMPORARY JAZZ or CONTEMPORARY JAZZ SPECIAL.

MARCUS MILLER JAZZ 1998–current *Signature on headstock.*
Similar to '75 JAZZ (see listing in earlier Japan Replica Jazz models section), except:
- Fretted bound maple neck only, block markers; Marcus Miller signature on headstock.
- Body sunburst, natural or white.
- Four controls (two volume, two tone), mini-switch and jack socket, all on pickguard.
- Revised-shape black laminated plastic pickguard.
- Heavier-duty four-saddle bridge/tailpiece.

NOEL REDDING JAZZ 1997 *Signature on headstock.*
Similar to 60s JAZZ (see listing in earlier Japan Replica Jazz models section), except:
- Noel Redding signature on headstock.
- Body sunburst only.

P-J *See earlier JAZZ SPECIAL listing.*

POWER JAZZ SPECIAL 1988–91 *Model name on graphite-face headstock.*
- Black maple neck with rosewood fingerboard, dot markers; 34-inch scale, 22 frets; truss-rod adjuster at body end; graphite-face headstock.
- Precision-style contoured double-cutaway body; various colours.
- One black eight-polepiece reversed split pickup and one black eight-polepiece straight pickup.
- Three controls (one volume, two tone), three-way selector and mini-switch, all on body; side-mounted jack socket; active circuit.
- No pickguard.
- Four-saddle bridge/tailpiece.
- Black-plated hardware

THE VENTURES JAZZ 1996 *The Ventures logo on headstock.*
- Maple neck with bound rosewood fingerboard, block markers; truss-rod adjuster at headstock end; The Ventures logo on black-face headstock.
- Contoured double-cutaway offset-waist body; blackburst only.
- Two white eight-polepiece straight pickups.
- Three controls (two volume, one tone).
- White pearl laminated plastic pickguard.
- Gold-plated hardware.
Optional Ventures logo for body.

JAPAN-MADE PRECISION MODELS
Japanese Precision models are divided into three sections: Japan Regular, Japan Replica and Japan Revised.

JAPAN REGULAR PRECISION MODELS
Listed here in alphabetical order are what we regard as Japan-made exported regular versions of the Precision.

STANDARD PRECISION 1988–91 *Modern-style 'thick' Fender headstock logo in silver.*
- Fretted maple neck or maple neck with rosewood fingerboard, dot markers; truss-rod adjuster at body end.
- Contoured double-cutaway body; sunburst or colours.
- One black eight-polepiece split pickup.
- Two controls (volume, tone) and jack socket, all on pickguard.
- White laminated plastic pickguard.
- Four-saddle bridge/tailpiece.

Replaced by Mexican-made version in 1991 (see STANDARD PRECISION listing in earlier Mexico Replica Precision models section).

JAPAN REPLICA PRECISION MODELS

Listed here in alphabetical/numerical order are the Japan-made exported replica versions of various standard U.S. Precision models (see earlier U.S. Regular Precision models section).

SQUIER VINTAGE SERIES '57 PRECISION 1982–83

Replica of 1957-period U.S. original (see PRECISION second version listing in earlier U.S. Regular Precision models section), but with white plastic pickguard. Small Squier Series logo on headstock. Replaced by Squier-branded version from 1983 (see later Squier main entry).

SQUIER VINTAGE SERIES '62 PRECISION 1982–83

Replica of 1962-period U.S. original (see PRECISION second version listing in earlier U.S. Regular Precision models section). Small Squier Series logo on headstock. Replaced by Squier-branded version from 1983 (see later Squier main entry).

'51 PRECISION 1992–98, 2003–current *Replica of 1951-period U.S. original (see PRECISION first version listing in earlier U.S. Regular Precision models section).*

50s PRECISION 1989–94 *Replica of 1950s-period U.S. original (see PRECISION second version listing in earlier U.S. Regular Precision models section), but with white plastic pickguard.*

60s PRECISION 1989–94 *Replica of 1960s-period U.S. original (see PRECISION second version listing in earlier U.S. Regular Precision models section).*

70s PRECISION 1992–93 *Replica of 1970s-period U.S. original (see PRECISION second version listing in earlier U.S. Regular Precision models section).*

JAPAN REVISED PRECISION MODELS

Listed here in alphabetical/numerical order are what we regard as the Japan-made exported revised and adapted versions of the Precision model.

ACOUSTIC/ELECTRIC PRECISION 1990–94 *F-hole, wooden-base bridge.*

■ Maple neck with fretless rosewood fingerboard (fretted option from 1993), dot markers; truss-rod adjuster at headstock end.
■ Semi-acoustic double-cutaway bound body with f-hole; sunburst or natural.
■ One black plain split pickup and piezo system in bridge.
■ Three controls (volume for magnetic pickup, tone for piezo pickup, balance) on body; side-mounted jack socket; active circuit.
■ No pickguard.
■ Single-saddle wooden-base bridge with through-body stringing.

AERODYNE CLASSIC PRECISION SPECIAL

2006–current *Model name on headstock.*
■ Maple neck with rosewood fingerboard, dot markers; truss-rod adjuster at body end; natural-, blue- or red-face headstock.
■ Contoured double-cutaway bound body with curved and figured top; natural, blue or red.
■ One black eight-polepiece split pickup and one black eight-polepiece straight pickup.
■ Three controls (two volume, one tone) on pickguard; side-mounted jack socket.
■ White laminated plastic pickguard.
■ Four-saddle bridge/tailpiece.

DONALD 'DUCK' DUNN PRECISION 1998 *Signature on headstock.*

Similar to 50s PRECISION (see listing in earlier Japan Replica Precision models listing), except:
■ Duck Dunn signature on headstock.
■ Body red only.
■ Gold anodised metal pickguard.

FOTO-FLAME 60s PRECISION 1994–96 *Fake figured wood finish on neck and body.*

Similar to 60s PRECISION (see listing in earlier Japan Replica Precision models section), except:
■ Foto Flame fake figured wood finish neck.
■ Foto Flame fake figured wood finish body; sunbursts or natural.
■ White or white pearl laminated plastic pickguard.

PRECISION LYTE 1989–95 *Revised-shape smaller body, four controls on body.*

■ Maple neck with rosewood fingerboard, dot markers; 34–inch scale, 22 frets; truss-rod adjuster at body end; coloured-face headstock.

- Revised-shape contoured double-cutaway smaller body; sunburst or colours.
- One black plain split pickup and one black plain straight pickup.
- Four controls (volume, two tone, balance) on body; side-mounted jack socket; active circuit.
- No pickguard.
- Four-saddle bridge/tailpiece.
- Gold-plated hardware.

Also blue or red Foto Flame fake figured wood finishes from 1992.

PRECISION LYTE DELUXE 1995–2001 *Model name on headstock, five controls on body, gold-plated hardware.*
Similar to PRECISION LYTE (see earlier listing), except:
- Truss-rod adjuster at headstock end.
- Body natural only.
- One black plain split pickup and one black plain pickup.
- Five controls (volume, three tone, balance) on body; side-mounted jack socket; active circuit.
- No pickguard.
- Four-saddle bridge with through-body stringing.
- Gold-plated hardware.

PRECISION LYTE STANDARD 1995–2001 *Model name on headstock, four controls on body, chrome-plated hardware.*
Similar to PRECISION LYTE (see earlier listing), except:
- Truss-rod adjuster at headstock end.
- Body various colours.
- Chrome-plated hardware.

STANDARD PRECISION SHORT-SCALE 1988–91
Shorter 32–inch scale neck.
Similar to STANDARD PRECISION (see listing in earlier Japan Regular Precision models section), except:
- 32–inch scale, 20 frets.

STEVE HARRIS SIGNATURE PRECISION 2001
Signature and Iron Maiden logo on headstock.
- Fretted maple neck, dot markers; truss-rod adjuster at body end; Steve Harris signature and Iron Maiden logo on headstock.
- Contoured double-cutaway body; blue only.
- One black eight-polepiece split pickup.
- Two controls (volume, tone) and jack socket, all on pickguard.
- Red mirror plastic pickguard.
- Four-saddle bridge/tailpiece.

STING SIGNATURE PRECISION 2001–current
Signature inlay at 12th fret.
Similar to '51 PRECISION (see listing in earlier Japan Regular Precision models section), except:
- Sting signature in pearl block at 12th fret.
- Body sunburst only.
- White plastic pickguard only.

'54 BLUE FLOWER PRECISION 2003 *Blue floral-pattern body finish.*
- Fretted maple neck, dot markers; truss-rod adjuster at body end.
- Contoured double-cutaway body; blue floral-pattern only.
- One four-polepiece small pickup.
- Two controls (volume, tone) on metal plate adjoining pickguard; side-mounted jack socket.
- Clear plastic pickguard.
- Two-saddle bridge with through-body stringing.

'54 PAISLEY PRECISION 2003 *Pink paisley-pattern body finish.*
- Fretted maple neck, dot markers; truss-rod adjuster at body end.
- Contoured double-cutaway body; pink paisley-pattern only.
- One four-polepiece small pickup.
- Two controls (volume, tone) on metal plate adjoining pickguard; side-mounted jack socket.
- Clear plastic pickguard.
- Two-saddle bridge with through-body stringing.

JAPAN-MADE OTHER MODELS
Selected other Japan-made exported Fender basses are listed here in alphabetical order of model name.

MUSTANG 2002–current *Replica of U.S. original (see MUSTANG listing in earlier U.S. Other models section).*

VI 1995–98 *Replica of U.S. original (see VI listing in earlier U.S. Other models section).*

FENDER KOREA

Many models made in Korea for Fender bear the Squier brandname (see later Squier entry). However, some have prominently featured the Fender logo and these are listed here. Each bass has 'Made In Korea' somewhere on the instrument.

KOREA-MADE JAZZ MODELS

JAZZ 24 2005–current *Revised-shape body, 24 frets.*
- Maple neck with rosewood fingerboard, dot markers; 34–inch scale, 24 frets; truss-rod adjuster at headstock end.
- Revised-shape contoured double-cutaway offset-waist body with figured top; sunbursts only.
- Two black eight-polepiece straight pickups.
- Three controls (volume, middle, balance), one dual-concentric control (treble/bass) and mini-switch, all on body; side-mounted jack socket; active circuit.
- No pickguard.
- Four-saddle bridge/tailpiece.

JAZZ 24 V 2007–current *Five strings, revised-shape body, 24 frets.*
Similar to JAZZ 24 (see earlier listing), except:
- Four-plus-one tuners with metal keys.
- Two black ten-polepiece straight pickups.
- Five-saddle bridge/tailpiece.

SQUIER SERIES JAZZ 1992–94 *Small Squier Series logo on headstock, controls and jack socket on white plastic pickguard.*
- Maple neck with rosewood fingerboard, dot markers; truss-rod adjuster at headstock end.
- Contoured double-cutaway offset-waist body; various colours.
- Two black eight-polepiece straight pickups.
- Three controls (two volume, one tone) and jack socket, all on pickguard.
- White plastic pickguard.
- Four-saddle bridge/tailpiece.
Replaced by Mexican-made version in 1994 (see listing in Mexico Replica Jazz models section).

KOREA-MADE PRECISION MODELS

SQUIER SERIES PRECISION 1992–94 *Small Squier Series logo on headstock.*
- Maple neck with rosewood fingerboard, dot markers; truss-rod adjuster at headstock end.
- Contoured double-cutaway body; various colours.

- One black eight-polepiece split pickup.
- Two controls (volume, tone) and jack socket, all on pickguard.
- White plastic pickguard.
- Four-saddle bridge/tailpiece.
Replaced by Mexican-made version in 1994 (see listing in Mexico Replica Precision models section).
Also active version (1992–94).

Other basses produced by Fender include:

U.S.A.
American Deluxe Zone 2001–06
Bass V five-string 1965–70
Bullet 1982–83
Coronado series 1966–71
HM series 1990–92
JP-90 1990–94
Musicmaster 1970–81
Prodigy Active 1991–94
Roscoe Beck 2004–current
Roscoe Beck V five-string 1995–2006
Stu Hamm Urge Signature 1995–99
Stu Hamm Urge II 1999–current

Mexico
Deluxe Zone 2001–06
Dimension 2004–06
Stu Hamm Urge Standard 1993–99

Japan
Jaguar 2006–current
Performer 1985–86
Prophecy series 1993–94
Stu Hamm Urge 1993–94

FENDER SERIAL NUMBERS

Depending on the production period, serial numbers can be located on the bass's backplate, neckplate, or on the front or back of the headstock.

Serial numbers should be regarded merely as a guide to dating, and ideally the production year should be confirmed by other age-related aspects of the individual instrument. As usual with mass-manufacturers, Fender does not assign serial numbers in exact chronological order, and components that bear the numbers – such as neckplates – were not used in strict rotation. As a result, apparent discrepancies and contradictions of as much as several years can and do occur.

The numbers we show in the tables represent the bulk of Fender's U.S., Mexican, and Japanese production, although there have been and continue to be various anomalies, odd series, special prefixes, and so on, but these have no overall dating relevance and are not listed. Also excluded are the series used on vintage replica reissues, limited editions, signature instruments, and so on. These are specific to certain models and not directly pertinent to production year.

The listing here does not apply to Fenders that originate from countries other than the U.S., Mexico,

and Japan; others (and Squier-brand instruments) have their own various number series, which unfortunately do sometimes duplicate those in the U.S. system. Prefixes include YN for China and CN for Korea (meaning the Cort factory).

Any confusion has to be resolved by studying other aspects of the instruments to determine correct origin (often by a simple 'Made In...' stamp) and production dates.

Fender Japan production commenced in 1982 and the company has used a series of prefixes to indicate the year of manufacture. We must stress, however, that the information in the table shown here is approximate and, again, should be used as a general guide only.

Some Japanese series have been used beyond the production spans listed here, in particular the original A-, C- and G-prefix numbers. There was a reversion to an A prefix for recent production, but a simple change from 'Made In Japan' to 'Crafted In Japan' somewhere on the bass helps to differentiate between the two sets of numbers.

Again, please bear in mind the need for caution in dating a Fender – and indeed most other basses – by using the serial number alone.

US number series	Approximate year(s)				
Up to 6,000	1951–54	100,000s to 200,000s	1966–67	N4 + 5/6 digits	1994–95
Up to 10,000 (4 or 5	1954–56	200,000s	1968	N5 + 5/6 digits	1995–96
digits, inc. 0 or – prefix)		200,000s to 300,000s	1969–70	N6 + 5/6 digits	1996–97
10,000s (4 or 5 digits,	1955–56	300,000s	1971–72	N7 + 5/6 digits	1997–98
inc. 0 or – prefix)		300,000s to 500,000s	1973	N8 + 5/6 digits	1998–99
10,000s to 20,000s	1957	400,000s to 500,000s	1974–75	N9 + 5/6 digits	1999–2000
(5 or 6 digits, inc. 0 or – prefix)		500,000s to 700,000s	1976	DZ0 + 5/6 digits	2000
20,000s to 30,000s	1958	800,000s to 900,000s	1979–81	Z0 + 5/6 digits	2000–01
(5 or 6 digits, inc. 0 or – prefix)		76 or S6 + 5 digits	1976	DZ1 + 5/6 digits	2001
30,000s to 40,000s	1959	S7 or S8 + 5 digits	1977	Z1 + 5/6 digits	2001–02
40,000s to 50,000s	1960	S7, S8 or S9 + 5 digits	1978	DZ2 + 5/6 digits	2002
50,000s to 70,000s	1961	S9 or E0 + 5 digits	1979	Z2 + 5/6 digits	2002–03
60,000s to 90,000s	1962	S9, E0 or E1 + 5 digits	1980–81	DZ3 + 5/6 digits	2003
80,000s to 90,000s	1963	E1, E2 or E3 + 5 digits	1982	Z3+ 5/6 digits	2003–04
Up to L10,000 (L + 5 digits)	1963	E2 or E3 + 5 digits	1983	DZ4 + 5/6 digits	2004
L10,000s to L20,000s	1963	E3 or E4 + 5 digits	1984–87	Z4 + 5/6 digits	2004–05
(L + 5 digits)		E4 + 5 digits	1987	DZ5 + 5/6 digits	2005
L20,000s to L50,000s	1964	E4 or E8 + 5 digits	1988	Z5 + 5/6 digits	2005–06
(L + 5 digits)		E8 or E9 + 5 digits	1989–90	DZ6 + 5/6 digits	2006
L50,000s to L90,000s	1965	E9 or N9 + 5 digits	1990–91	Z6 + 5/6 digits	2006–07
(L + 5 digits)		N0 + 5 digits	1990–91	DZ7 + 5/6 digits	2007
100,000s	1965	N1 + 5/6 digits	1991–92	Z7 + 5/6 digits	2007–08
		N2 + 5/6 digits	1992–93		
		N3 + 5/6 digits	1993–94		

Mexico number series	Approximate year(s)	'Made In Japan' number series	Approximate year(s)	Q + 6 digits	1993–94
				S + 6 digits	1994–95
MN1 + 5/6 digits	1991–92	JV + 5 digits	1982–84	T + 6 digits	1994–95
MN2 + 5/6 digits	1992–93	SQ + 5 digits	1983–84	U + 6 digits	1995–96
MN3 + 5/6 digits	1993–94	E + 6 digits	1984–87	V + 6 digits	1996–97
MN4 + 5/6 digits	1994–95	A + 6 digits	1985–86, 1997–current		
MN5 + 5/6 digits	1995–96	B + 6 digits	1985–86	'Crafted In Japan' number series	Approximate year(s)
MN6 + 5/6 digits	1996–97	C + 6 digits	1985–86		
MN7 + 5/6 digits	1997–98	F + 6 digits	1986–87	A + 6 digits	1997–98
MN8 + 5/6 digits	1998–99	G + 6 digits	1987–88	B + 6 digits	1998–99
MN9 + 5/6 digits	1999–2000	H + 6 digits	1988–89	O + 5/6 digits	1997–2000
MZ0 + 5/6 digits	2000–01	I + 6 digits	1989–90	P + 5/6 digits	1999–2002
MZ1 + 5/6 digits	2001–02	J + 6 digits	1989–90	Q + 5/6 digits	2002–04
MZ2 + 5/6 digits	2002–03	K + 6 digits	1990–91	R + 5/6 digits	2004–05
MZ3 + 5/6 digits	2003–04	L + 6 digits	1991–92	S + 5/6 digits	2006–07
MZ4 + 5/6 digits	2004–05	M + 6 digits	1992–93		
MZ5 + 5/6 digits	2005–06	N + 6 digits	1993–94		
MZ6 + 5/6 digits	2006–07	O + 6 digits	1993–94		
MZ7 + 5/6 digits	2007–08	P + 6 digits	1993–94		

GIBSON

U.S.

EB-2 1958–61, 1964–70 *Semi-acoustic twin-cutaway body, one pickup.*
■ Glued-in neck with rosewood fingerboard, dot markers; 30.5-inch scale, 20 frets; truss-rod adjuster at headstock end; two-a-side tuners with rear-facing plastic keys (horizontal metal type from c1960).
■ Hollow twin-cutaway bound body with two f-holes; sunburst, natural or colours.
■ One plastic-cover (metal-cover from c1964) four-polepiece pickup.
■ Two controls (volume, tone) and tone pushbutton switch (from c1959), all on body; front-mounted jack socket.
■ Black laminated plastic pickguard.
■ Single-saddle bridge/tailpiece.
Also EB-2D with two pickups (1966–72).

EB-3 1961–79 *Solid bevelled-edge double-cutaway body, two pickups.*
■ Glued-in neck with rosewood fingerboard (bound c1969–72), dot markers; 30.5-inch scale, 20 frets (some with 19 or 21 frets from c1969); truss-rod adjuster at headstock end; two-a-side tuners with

metal keys; slotted headstock (c1969–72).
■ Solid bevelled-edge double-cutaway body; red, brown, natural or white.
■ One plastic-cover (metal-cover from c1962) four-polepiece pickup plus smaller metal-cover four-polepiece pickup.
■ Four controls (two volume, two tone) and four-way rotary selector, all on body; front-mounted jack socket.
■ Black laminated plastic pickguard.
■ Single-saddle bridge/tailpiece (four-saddle bridge/tailpiece from c1974).
Also EB-3L with 34.5-inch scale (1970–74).

THUNDERBIRD II first version (reverse) 1963–65
Through-neck, solid reversed-offset body with longer right horn, one pickup.
■ Through-neck with rosewood fingerboard, dot markers; 34.5-inch scale, 20 frets; truss-rod adjuster at headstock end; four-in-line tuners with metal keys.
■ Solid reversed-offset body with raised through-neck centre section; sunburst or colours.
■ One metal-cover plain pickup.
■ Two controls (volume, tone) on body; front-mounted jack socket.
■ White laminated plastic pickguard with stylised bird emblem.
■ Four-saddle bridge, tailpiece.

THUNDERBIRD II second version (non-reverse)

1965–69 Glued-in neck, solid double-cutaway body with shallow rounded horns, one pickup.

- Glued-in neck with rosewood fingerboard, dot markers; 34.5–inch scale, 20 frets; truss-rod adjuster at headstock end; four-in-line tuners with metal keys.
- Solid double-cutaway body; sunburst or colours.
- One metal-cover plain pickup.
- Two controls (volume, tone) on body; front-mounted jack socket.
- White laminated plastic pickguard with stylised bird emblem.
- Four-saddle bridge, tailpiece.

THUNDERBIRD II 1983–84 *Reissue based on first version (reverse) 1963–65 period original (see earlier listing).*

THUNDERBIRD IV first version (reverse) 1963–65
Through-neck, solid reversed-offset body with longer right horn, two pickups.
Similar to THUNDERBIRD II first version, except:
- Two metal-cover plain pickups.
- Three controls (two volume, one tone).

THUNDERBIRD IV second version (non-reverse)

1965–69 Glued-in neck, solid double-cutaway body with shallow rounded horns, two pickups.
Similar to THUNDERBIRD II second version, except:
- Two metal-cover plain pickups.
- Three controls (two volume, one tone).

THUNDERBIRD IV third version (reverse)

1987–current Pickups with no surrounds, black-plated hardware.
Similar to Thunderbird IV first version, except:
- Pickups with no surrounds.
- Four-saddle bridge/tailpiece.
- Black-plated hardware.

THUNDERBIRD 76 1976–77 *Red/white/blue bird emblem, four-saddle bridge/tailpiece.*
Similar to Thunderbird IV first version, except:
- Sunburst, natural or colours.
- Red/white/blue stylised bird emblem (commemorating U.S. Bicentennial).
- Four-saddle bridge/tailpiece.

THUNDERBIRD 79 1979 *Four-saddle bridge/tailpiece.*
Similar to Thunderbird IV first version, except:

- Sunburst, natural or black.
- Four-saddle bridge/tailpiece.

THUNDERBIRD STUDIO 2005–current *Solid reversed-offset body with no raised centre section.*
Similar to Thunderbird IV first version, except:
- Glued-in neck.
- Solid reversed-offset body with no raised centre section; black or red.
- Pickups with no surrounds,
- Four-saddle bridge/tailpiece.
Also five-string version (2005–current).

Other basses produced by Gibson include:
Electric Bass violin-shape body 1953–58
EB-0 first version slab body 1959–61
EB-0 second version bevelled-edge body 1961–74
EB-1 violin shape body 1969–71
EB-4L 1972–73
EB-650 and **EB-750** semis 1992–93
Explorer 1984–87
Flying V 1981–82
Grabber/G-1 1974–82
G-3 1975–82
Les Paul Signature semi-acoustic 1973–79
Les Paul Triumph 1971–79
LPB Les Paul series 1992–
L-9S/Ripper 1973–82
Melody Maker 1968–70
Nikki Sixx Signature Thunderbird 2000–
Q-80/Q-90 Combo 1986–92
RD series 1977–82
Victory series 1981–87
IV and **V** 1987–89

HOFNER

Germany

500/1 1956–current *Semi-acoustic violin-shape body.*
- Glued-in neck with rosewood fingerboard (bound from c1963), dot markers; 30–inch scale, 22 frets; truss-rod adjuster at headstock end; two-a-side tuners with plastic keys.
- Hollow violin-shape bound body; sunburst only.
- Two pickups (close-spaced at neck c1957–61).
- Four controls (two volume, two tone) on oval plastic plate (volume, tone and three slide- switches on

rectangular plastic plate from c1957); side-mounted jack socket.

■ Tortoiseshell plastic (white pearl plastic from c1961) pickguard.

■ Four-saddle bridge, tailpiece.

Also 500/1B and 500/1M, each with active circuit.

Also 500/1 CAVERN, reissue based on 1961-period original.

Also 500/1 VINTAGE '62, reissue based on 1962-period original.

Also 500/1 VINTAGE '63, reissue based on 1963-period original.

Also 500/1 40th ANNIVERSARY, limited edition of 400.

Other basses produced by Hofner include:
S7B 1978–84
S9B 1982–85
185 1962–83
500/2 semi-acoustic 1965–70
500/3 semi-acoustic, known as **Senator** in U.K. 1960–64
500/5 semi-acoustic known as **President** in U.K. 1957–79
500/7 semi-acoustic known as **Verithin** in U.K. 1963–70

IBANEZ

Japan

MUSICIAN MC-900 1979 *Through-neck, solid contoured double-cutaway body, two pickups, five controls, three-way selector and mini-switch.*

■ Through-neck with ebony fingerboard, dot markers; 34–inch scale, 22 frets; truss-rod adjuster at headstock end; two-a-side tuners with metal keys.

■ Solid contoured double-cutaway body; natural only.

■ Two four-polepiece pickups.

■ Five controls (volume, four tone), three-way selector and mini-switch, all on body; front-mounted jack socket; active circuit.

■ Four-saddle bridge/tailpiece.
Replaced by MC-924 in late 1979.

Other basses produced by Ibanez include:
Artcore series 2004–
ATK first series 1995–
ATK second series 2007–current
BTB series 1999–current
Doug Wimbish Signature series 1999–
Ergodyne series 1996–current

Gary Willis Signature series 1999–
Iceman series 2004–current
Musician series 1979–
Roadgear series 2004–current
Roadstar series 1982–
Roadster series 1979–
Soundgear series 1988–current
Studio series 1979–
TR Expressionist series 1997–

MUSIC MAN

U.S.

MUSIC MAN 1976–84

STINGRAY 1976–84 *Solid slab double-cutaway body, circular pickguard, controls on metal plate, one string-guide on G and D strings.*

■ Bolt-on fretted maple neck or maple neck with rosewood fingerboard (fretless ebony option), dot markers; 34–inch scale, 21 frets; truss-rod adjuster at headstock end; three-and-one tuners with metal keys; one string-guide (on G and D strings); three-screw neckplate (four-screw from 1980).

■ Solid slab double-cutaway body; sunburst, natural or colours.

■ One eight-polepiece pickup.

■ Three controls (volume, two tone) and jack socket, all on metal plate; active circuit (optional, later standard).

■ Black or white laminated plastic pickguard.

■ Four-saddle bridge with through-body stringing (bridge/tailpiece from 1980); individual string-mutes.

Other basses produced by Music Man include:
Cutlass 1983
Sabre 1976–84

ERNIE BALL MUSIC MAN 1984–current

STINGRAY 1984–current *Solid contoured double-cutaway body, circular pickguard, controls on metal plate, one string-guide on D and A strings.*

■ Bolt-on fretted maple neck (later maple neck with maple fingerboard) or maple neck with rosewood fingerboard (fretless rosewood option, later pau ferro), dot markers; 34–inch scale, 21 frets; truss-rod adjuster at headstock end (later at body end); three-and-one tuners with metal keys; one string-guide (on D and A strings); four-screw neckplate (later six-screw).

- Solid contoured double-cutaway body; sunburst, natural or colours.
- One eight-polepiece pickup (also two eight-polepiece pickups (HH) or one eight-polepiece pickup and one four-polepiece pickup (HS) from 2005).
- Three controls (volume, two tone) and jack socket, all on metal plate or four controls (volume, three tone) on metal plate and side-mounted jack socket; five-way selector (on two-pickup versions) on body; active circuit.
- Clear, black, black or white or tortoiseshell or black pearloid or white pearloid or abalone laminated plastic pickguard.
- Four-saddle bridge/tailpiece; individual string-mutes (later removed).

Piezo pickup-equipped bridge plus balance control option (from 1999).

STINGRAY 5 1988–current *Five strings, solid contoured double-cutaway body, one pickup.*

- Bolt-on maple neck with maple or rosewood fingerboard (fretless rosewood option, later pau ferro), dot markers; 34–inch scale, 22 frets; truss-rod adjuster at body end; four-and-one tuners with metal keys; six-screw neckplate.
- Solid contoured double-cutaway body; sunburst, natural or colours.
- One ten-polepiece pickup (two eight-polepiece pickups (HH) or one eight-polepiece pickup and one four-polepiece pickup (HS) options from 2005).
- Four controls (volume, three tone) and three-way selector (five-way selector on two-pickup versions), all on pickguard; side-mounted jack socket; active circuit.
- Black or white or tortoiseshell or black pearloid or white pearloid or abalone laminated plastic pickguard.
- Five-saddle bridge/tailpiece.

Piezo pickup-equipped bridge plus balance control option (from 1999).

STINGRAY 20th ANNIVERSARY 1996
Commemorative headstock logo, controls on body.
Similar to STINGRAY (see earlier listing), except:
- Commemorative headstock logo.
- Body with figured maple top; natural with red back only.

- Four controls (volume, three tone) on body; side-mounted jack socket.
- Tortoiseshell laminated plastic pickguard.

STINGRAY 5 20th ANNIVERSARY 2007
Commemorative headstock logo, controls on body, five strings.
Similar to STINGRAY 5 (see earlier listing), except:
- Commemorative headstock logo; five-screw neckplate.
- Body with figured maple top; sunburst only.
- One ten-polepiece pickup (also two eight-polepiece pickups (HH) or one eight-polepiece pickup and one four-polepiece pickup (HS) options).
- Four controls (volume, three tone) and five-way selector, all on body.

STINGRAY 30th ANNIVERSARY 2005 *Commemorative headstock logo.*
Similar to STINGRAY (see earlier listing), except:
- Bolt-on maple neck with rosewood fingerboard; commemorative headstock logo; commemorative neckplate.
- Mahogany body; red only.
- Four controls (volume, three tone) on metal plate; side-mounted jack socket; active circuit.
- Four-saddle bridge with through-body stringing.

STINGRAY NAMM 100th ANNIVERSARY 2001
Commemorative medallion on headstock.
Similar to STINGRAY (see earlier listing), except:
- Bolt-on graphite neck with rosewood fingerboard; commemorative medallion on headstock.
- Silver only.
- Four controls (volume, three tone) on metal plate; side-mounted jack socket; active circuit.
- Black pearloid laminated plastic pickguard.
- Four-saddle bridge with through-body stringing.
Limited edition of 100.

Other basses produced by Ernie Ball Music Man include:
Bongo 2003–current
Sabre 1984–91
Silhouette six-string 1991–current
Sterling 1994–current
S.U.B. 2003–07
S.U.B. 5 five-string 2003–07
S.U.B. Sterling 2004–07

PEAVEY

CIRRUS 4 1997–current *Logo on headstock, C at 12th fret.*

- Through-neck with pau ferro fingerboard (maple option from 2001), no markers, C logo at 12th fret; 35–inch scale, 24 frets; truss-rod adjuster at headstock end; two-a-side tuners with metal keys.
- Solid contoured double-cutaway body; natural only.
- Two black plain active pickups.
- Five controls (volume, three tone, balance) on body; side-mounted jack socket; active circuit.
- Four-saddle bridge/tailpiece.
- Gold-plated hardware.

Also five- and six-string versions (1997–current).

CIRRUS 4 bolt-on 2003–current *Logo on headstock, C at 12th fret, bolt-on neck.*

Similar to CIRRUS 4 (see earlier listing), except:

- Bolt-on walnut neck with wenge or pau ferro fingerboard; 34–inch scale, 24 frets.
- Four-saddle bridge with through-body stringing.
- Black-plated hardware (gold-plated from 2005).

Also five-string version with 35–inch scale (2003–current).

CIRRUS BXP 4 2004–current *Through-neck, through-body stringing*

Similar to CIRRUS 4 (see earlier listing), except:

- Through-neck with pau ferro fingerboard.
- Four-saddle bridge with through-body stringing.

Also five-string version.

Other basses produced by Peavey include:
Axcelerator 2–T 1996–
Axcelerator 6 six-string 1997–
B-Quad series 1994–
CyberBass 1994–
Dyna-Base 1985–
Fury II 1998–
Fury series 2001–
G-Bass 1998–
G-V 1998–
Grind Bass series 2002–
Jack Daniels (2005–
Liberator JT-84 2007–
Midibase 1992–
Milestone series 1998–
Millennium series 2000–
Palaedium 1991–

RJ IV 1991–
TL series 1989–
T-40 1977–
Zodiac U.S.A. series 2005–

RICKENBACKER

U.S.

4001 1961–86 *Through-neck, solid double-cutaway bound body, through-neck, triangle markers, two pickups.*

- Through-neck with bound rosewood fingerboard, triangle markers; 33.5–inch scale, 20 frets; truss-rod adjuster at headstock end; two-a-side tuners with metal keys.
- Solid double-cutaway bound body; sunburst, natural or colours.
- Two pickups.
- Four controls (two volume, two tone) and three-way selector, all on pickguard; side-mounted jack socket.
- White plastic pickguard (later black plastic option).
- Four-saddle bridge/tailpiece.

Also 4001FL fretless version.

4001CS CHRIS SQUIRE 1991–2000 *Signature on pickguard.*

Similar to 1960s-period 4001S (see earlier listing), except:

- Custom-shape neck; unbound padauk fingerboard, dot markers.
- Unbound body; cream only.
- Chris Squire signature and 'Limited Edition' on pickguard.

4001S 1961–69 *Solid double-cutaway unbound body, through-neck, dot markers, two pickups.*

Similar to 4001 (see earlier listing), except:

- Unbound rosewood fingerboard, dot markers.
- Unbound body.

Known as Model 1999 in UK (1964–69).

Also 4001SF fretless version.
Also 4001V63, reissue based on 1963-period original.

Other basses produced by Rickenbacker include:
2020 Hamburg 1992–97
2030 Hamburg 1984–92
2030GF Glenn Frey 1992–95
2050 El Dorado 1984–92

2060 El Dorado 1992–97
3000 1975–84
3001 1975–84
4000 1957–84
4002 1976–85
4003 1979–current
4003S 1981–95
4003S/5 five-string 1986–
4003S/8 eight-string 1986–
4004C Cheyenne 1993–current
4004L Laredo 1994–current
4005 1965–84
4005S (**3261** in U.K.) 1965–69
4005/6 1965–78
4008 eight-string 1975–84

SPECTOR

U.S.

NS-2 first version 1979–90 *Through-neck, solid double-cutaway concave back/convex front body, two pickups, four controls, two mini-switches.*

- Through-neck with rosewood fingerboard, dot markers (later ornate); 34-inch scale, 24 frets; truss-rod adjuster at headstock end; two-a-side tuners with metal keys.
- Solid double-cutaway body, concave back/convex front; natural or colours.
- One split and one straight pickup.
- Four controls (volume, two tone, balance) and two mini-switches, all on body; side-mounted jack socket; active circuit.
- Four-saddle bridge/tailpiece.

NS-2 second version 1998–current *Through-neck, solid double-cutaway concave back/convex front body, two pickups, four controls.*
Similar to NS-2 first version (see earlier listing), except:
- Four controls (volume, two tone, balance) on body.

Other basses produced by Spector include:
U.S.
NS-1 1977–80
NS-1B 1982–85
NS-2J 1983–85
NS-JH6 six-string 2001–
SB-1 1975–79

SB-2 1976–79
SSD (Stuart Spector Design) **NS-4** 1992–98
SSD (Stuart Spector Design) **NS-5** five-string 1993–98

Czech Republic
Europe series 2004–current
ReBop 2002–04
SSD (Stuart Spector Design) **NS-4CR** 1994–98
SSD (Stuart Spector Design) **NS-5CR** five-string 1994–98

Korea
Legend 2004–06
NS series 1987–90
SSD (Stuart Spector Design) **NS-94** 1994–98
SSD (Stuart Spector Design) **NS-95** five-string 1994–98
NS-2004 1998–2002
NS-2005 five-string 1998–2002
Q4 Pro 1999–2004
Q5 Pro five-string 1999–2004
Q6 Pro 1999–2004

SQUIER

The first instruments with the Squier brand appeared in the early 1980s and were Japanese-made Fenders exported into Europe, but soon they were sold elsewhere and later made elsewhere.

Fender's policy is that Squier caters for lower pricepoints, maintaining the company's ever-expanding market coverage – but not by cheapening the Fender name itself.

The Squier logo, supported by a small but important 'by Fender' line, appeared on an increasing number of models during its first decade. At first these originated in Japan, but escalating production costs meant a move to cheaper manufacturing sources. Korea came on line in 1985, and India made a brief appearance in the late 1980s before returning to the roster in 2007.

Fender's facility in Mexico helped out too in the early 1990s, and more recently China, Indonesia, and India have entered the picture, providing entry-level basses with the kudos of a Fender connection. Each Squier bass should have the relevant country of origin somewhere on the instrument.

The continuing success story of Squier makes this a very important support brand for Fender, with a

level of design and build quality that regularly
exceeds its apparent status as a second-string line.

JAZZ

**Features common to all Squier Jazz models, unless
stated otherwise:**

- Bolt-on neck.
- Maple neck with unbound rosewood fingerboard.
- Dot markers.
- 34–inch scale, 20 frets.
- Truss-rod adjuster at headstock end.
- Four in-line tuners with metal keys.
- Four-screw neckplate.
- Contoured double-cutaway offset-waist unbound solid
  body.
- Two black eight-polepiece straight pickups.
- Three controls (two volume, one tone) and jack
  socket, all on metal plate adjoining pickguard.
- Four-saddle bridge/tailpiece.
- Nickel- or chrome-plated hardware.

SQUIER JAZZ MODELS

Squier Jazz models are divided into three sections:
Squier Regular, Squier Replica, and Squier Revised.

SQUIER REGULAR JAZZ MODELS

Listed here in alphabetical order are what we regard as
Squier regular versions of the Jazz model.

AFFINITY J-BASS 2004–current *Model name and Affinity
Series logo on headstock.*
- Body various colours.
- White laminated plastic pickguard.

SILVER SERIES JAZZ 1992–94 *Silver Series logo on
headstock.*
- Body sunburst or colours.
- White or black laminated plastic pickguard

STANDARD JAZZ 1985–current *See common features.*
- Truss-rod adjuster at body end on some examples.
- Body sunburst or colours.
- White laminated plastic pickguard.

VINTAGE MODIFIED JAZZ 2006–current *Fretted black
bound maple neck, black block markers.*
- Fretted black bound maple neck, black block markers.
- Body natural only.
- Black laminated plastic pickguard only.

SQUIER REPLICA JAZZ MODELS

Listed here in alphabetical order are Squier replica
versions of various standard U.S. Jazz models (see U.S.
Regular Jazz models in earlier Fender entry).

VINTAGE '62 JAZZ 1983–85 *Replica of 1962-period
U.S. original (see JAZZ second version listing in U.S.
Regular Jazz models section in earlier Fender main entry).
Replaced Fender Squier Series version (see listing in
Japan Replica Jazz models section in earlier Fender main
entry). Truss-rod adjuster at body end.*

SQUIER REVISED JAZZ MODELS

Listed here in alphabetical order are what we regard as
Squier revised and adapted versions of the Jazz model.

AFFINITY J-BASS V 2007–current *Five strings, model
name and Affinity Series logo on headstock.*
Similar to AFFINITY J-BASS (see listing in earlier Squier
Regular Jazz models section), except:
- Five in-line tuners with metal keys.
- Two black ten-polepiece straight pickups.
- Five-saddle bridge/tailpiece.

DELUXE ACTIVE JAZZ V 2007–current *Five strings, four
controls and mini-switch on body.*
- Maple neck with synthetic fingerboard, dot markers;
  four-plus-one tuners with metal keys.
- Body sunburst only.
- Two black plain straight pickups.
- Three controls (volume, middle, balance), one dual-
  concentric control (treble/bass) and mini-switch, all on
  body; side-mounted jack socket; active circuit.
- No pickguard.
- Five-saddle bridge/tailpiece.

FRANK BELLO JAZZ 2007–current *Skull inlay at 12th
fret, skull graphic on black body.*
- Skull inlay at 12th fret; black-face headstock.
- Body black with large skull graphic.
- One black eight-polepiece split pickup and one black
  eight-polepiece straight pickup.
- Two controls (vol) on body; side-mounted jack socket.
- No pickguard.

VINTAGE MODIFIED JAZZ FRETLESS 2006–current
Fretless fingerboard, no pickguard.
- Maple neck with fretless synthetic fingerboard, no dot
  markers.

■ Body sunburst only.
■ No pickguard.

PRECISION

Features common to all Squier Precision models, unless stated otherwise:

■ Bolt-on neck.
■ Maple neck with unbound rosewood fingerboard.
■ Dot markers.
■ 34–inch scale, 20 frets.
■ Truss-rod adjuster at headstock end.
■ Four in-line tuners with metal keys.
■ Four-screw neckplate.
■ Contoured double-cutaway unbound solid body.
■ One black eight-polepiece split pickup.
■ Two controls (volume, tone) and jack socket, all on pickguard.
■ Four-saddle bridge/tailpiece.
■ Nickel- or chrome-plated hardware.

SQUIER PRECISION MODELS

Squier Precision models are divided into three sections: Squier Regular, Squier Replica and Squier Revised.

SQUIER REGULAR PRECISION MODELS

Listed here in alphabetical order are what we regard as Squier regular versions of the Precision model.

AFFINITY P-BASS 1997–current *Model name and Affinity Series logo on headstock.*

■ Body sunburst or colours.
■ White plastic pickguard.
Also 20th ANNIVERSARY version with commemorative neckplate (2002).

POPULAR/STANDARD PRECISION 1984–85 *Gold Squier headstock logo.*

■ Truss-rod adjuster at body end.
■ Body sunburst or black.
■ White or black laminated plastic pickguard.

SILVER SERIES PRECISION 1992–94 *Silver Series logo on headstock.*

■ Body sunburst or colours.
■ White or black laminated plastic pickguard.

STANDARD PRECISION 1988–98 *See common features.*

■ Maple neck with maple or rosewood fingerboard; truss-rod adjuster at body end on some examples.
■ Body sunburst or colours.
■ White or white laminated plastic pickguard.

TRADITIONAL P-BASS 1996 *Model name on headstock.*

■ Body various colours.
■ White plastic pickguard.
Re-named AFFINITY from 1997.

VINTAGE MODIFIED PRECISION 2006–current *Duncan Designed logo on pickup.*

■ Body white only.
■ One black eight-polepiece split pickup with Duncan Designed logo.
■ Black laminated plastic pickguard only.

SQUIER REPLICA PRECISION MODELS

Listed here in alphabetical order are Squier replica versions of various standard U.S. Precisions (see U.S. Regular Precision models in earlier Fender main entry).

VINTAGE '57 PRECISION 1983–85 *Replica of 1957-period U.S. original (see PRECISION second version listing in U.S. Regular Precision models section in earlier Fender main entry), but with white plastic pickguard. Replaced Fender Squier Series version (see listing in Japan Replica Precision models section in earlier Fender main entry). Truss-rod adjuster at body end.*

VINTAGE '62 PRECISION 1983–85 *Replica of 1962-period U.S. original (see PRECISION second version listing in U.S. Regular Precision models section in earlier Fender main entry). Replaced Fender Squier Series version (see listing in Japan Replica Precision models section in earlier Fender main entry). Truss-rod adjuster at body end.*

SQUIER REVISED PRECISION MODELS

Listed here in alphabetical order what we regard as Squier revised and adapted versions of the Precision model.

AFFINITY P-BASS SPECIAL 1998 *Black split pickup and black straight pickup, three controls on pickguard, side-mounted jack socket, Affinity Series logo on headstock.*

■ Jazz-style neck.
■ Body black, red or white.

- One black eight-polepiece split pickup and one black eight-polepiece straight pickup..
- Three controls (two volume, one tone) on pickguard; side-mounted jack socket.
- White plastic pickguard.

AFFINITY P-BASS LIMITED EDITION 2003–04 *Grey-face headstock, black-plated hardware, Affinity Series logo on headstock.*
Similar to AFFINITY P-BASS (see listing in earlier Squier Regular Precision models section), except:
- Grey-face headstock.
- Body grey only.
- Black plastic pickguard.
- Black-plated hardware.

MIKE DIRNT PRECISION 2007–current *Enlarged Telecaster-style headstock, white star graphic on black body.*
- Body black with white star graphic.
- Two controls (volume, tone) on metal plate adjoining pickguard; side-mounted jack socket.
- White plastic pickguard.

PETE WENTZ PRECISION 2007–current *Signature on back of headstock, red bat graphic on black body.*
- Maple neck with maple fingerboard, black bat inlay at 12th fret; P-Bass on headstock; Pete Wentz signature on back of headstock.
- Body black with red bat graphic.
- One control (volume) and jack socket on pickguard.
- Red tortoiseshell laminated plastic pickguard.

PRO TONE PJ 1996–97 *Black split pickup and black straight pickup, three controls and jack socket on pickguard, Pro Tone logo on headstock.*
- Black-face headstock.
- Body black only.
- One black eight-polepiece split pickup and one black eight-polepiece straight pickup..
- Three controls (two volume, one tone) and jack socket, all on pickguard.
- Red tortoiseshell laminated plastic pickguard.

PRO TONE PRECISION V 1996–97 *Five strings, two plain large pickups, Pro Tone logo on headstock.*
- Five in-line tuners with metal keys.
- Body red only.
- Two black plain large pickups.

- Three controls (two volume, one tone) and jack socket, all on pickguard.
- White pearl laminated plastic pickguard.
- Five-saddle bridge/tailpiece.
- Gold-plated hardware.

STANDARD P-BASS SPECIAL *See later STANDARD PRECISION SPECIAL listing.*

STANDARD PRECISION SHORT-SCALE 1984–88 *Shorter 32–inch scale neck.*
Similar to STANDARD PRECISION (see listing in earlier Squier Regular Precision models section), except:
- 32–inch scale, 20 frets.

STANDARD PRECISION SPECIAL 1999–current *Black split pickup and black straight pickup, three controls on pickguard, side-mounted jack socket, Standard Series logo on headstock.*
- Jazz-style neck.
- Body sunburst or colours.
- One black eight-polepiece split pickup and one black eight-polepiece straight pickup.
- Three controls (two volume, one tone) on pickguard; side-mounted jack socket.
- White, black or tortoiseshell laminated plastic pickguard.
Known as P-BASS SPECIAL (1999–2000).

STANDARD PRECISION SPECIAL BLACK & CHROME 2004–current *Black body, chrome plastic pickguard, Standard Series logo on headstock.*
Similar to STANDARD PRECISION SPECIAL (see earlier listing), except:
- Black-face headstock.
- Body black only.
- Chrome plastic pickguard.

STANDARD PRECISION SPECIAL 5 2000–current *Five strings, two plain straight pickups, Standard Series logo on headstock.*
- Four-plus-one tuners with metal keys.
- Body sunburst or colours.
- Two black plain straight pickups.
- Three controls (two volume, one tone) and jack socket, all on pickguard.
- White, black or tortoiseshell laminated plastic pickguard.
- Five-saddle bridge/tailpiece.

VINTAGE MODIFIED PRECISION TB 2007–current
Enlarged Telecaster-style headstock, metal-cover split-polepiece pickup.
- Fretted maple neck.
- Body sunburst only.
- One metal-cover split-polepiece pickup.
- Two controls (volume, tone) on pickguard; side-mounted jack socket.
- Black laminated plastic pickguard.
- Two-saddle bridge with through-body stringing.

Based on FENDER TELECASTER second version (see listing in U.S. Other models section in earlier Fender main entry).

Other basses produced by Squier include:
Bronco 1998–current
Bullet 1983–88
HM series 1989–92
MB series 1993–current
Musicmaster 1997–98

STEINBERGER

U.S.

L-2 1980–84 *Synthetic one-piece headless neck/mini straight-sided body, body-top fixing bolts on front, two active pickups.*
- Synthetic one-piece headless neck/body with synthetic fingerboard, dot markers; 34–inch scale, 24 frets; tuners at body end.
- Solid straight-sided mini synthetic body (with separate top, fixing bolts on front); black only.
- Two active plain pickups.
- Three controls (two volume, one tone) all on body; side-mounted jack socket.
- Four-saddle bridge/tailpiece with tuners.
- Strap-holder bracket on body back.
- Side-mounted hinged leg-rest.
- Black-plated hardware.

Also active circuit option (1982–84).

L-2/5 1982–84 *Synthetic one-piece headless neck/mini straight-sided body, body-top fixing bolts on front, two active pickups, five strings.*
Similar to L-2, except:
- Five strings.
- Five-saddle bridge/tailpiece with tuners.

Also active circuit option.

Other basses produced by Steinberger include:
U.S.
H-1 and **H-2** 1980–82
L-1 1980–84
XB 1998–
XL series 1984–
XM-2 1986–93
XQ series 1990–
XS Synapse series 2005–

Japan
XP series 1984–90

Korea
XT-2 Spirit series 1993–

WARWICK

Germany

Features common to all Warwick models, unless stated otherwise:
- Dot markers.
- 34-inch scale, 24 frets.
- Truss-rod adjuster at headstock end.
- Two-a-side tuners with metal keys.
- Solid body.
- All controls on body.
- Side-mounted jack socket.

CORVETTE
CORVETTE DOUBLE-BUCK ($$) 2005–current
Corvette $$ on headstock.
Similar to CORVETTE PRO-LINE (see later listing), except:
- Two black eight-polepiece pickups.
- Four controls (volume, balance, two tone) and two mini-switches; active circuit.
- Black-plated hardware.

Also five-string version (2005–current).
Also six-string version (2008–current).

CORVETTE DOUBLE-BUCK ($$) NT 2007–current
Corvette NT on headstock.
Similar to CORVETTE DOUBLE BUCK (see earlier listing), except:
- Through-neck.

Also five-string version (2007–current).

WARWICK CORVETTE

CORVETTE ALTUS 1998 *One black eight-polepiece pickup.*
Similar to CORVETTE PRO LINE (see later listing), except:
- One black eight-polepiece pickup.
- Four controls (volume, three tone).
- Gold-plated hardware.

Also five-string version (1998).
Model name changed to CORVETTE FNA in 1998, later known as FNA.

CORVETTE FNA *See earlier CORVETTE ALTUS listing.*

CORVETTE HOT ROD LTD 2005 *Maple fingerboard, planet markers.*
Similar to CORVETTE PRO LINE (see later listing), except:
- Maple fingerboard, planet markers.
- Natural only.
- Two black plain split pickups (one reversed).
- Two dual-concentric controls (volume/balance, treble/bass) and one control (middle).
- Black-plated hardware.

Also five-string version (2005).
Limited edition of 250.
Custom Shop from 2006.

CORVETTE PRO LINE 1992–2007 *Model name on headstock.*
- Bolt-on neck with wenge fingerboard (fretless ebony option), no markers.
- Contoured, double-cutaway body; sunburst, natural or colours.
- Two black plain pickups.
- Two controls (volume, balance) and one dual-concentric control (treble/bass); active circuit.
- Four-saddle bridge, tailpiece.
- Chrome- or gold-plated hardware.

Also five-string version (1992–2007).
Also six-string version (1994–2007).

CORVETTE STANDARD (STD) 1995–current *Model name on headstock.*
Similar to CORVETTE PRO LINE (see earlier listing), except:
- Active or passive circuit.
- Chrome-plated hardware.

Also five-string version (1995–current).
Also six-string version (1997–current).

CORVETTE TARANIS 2007–current *Model name on headstock.*
Similar to CORVETTE PRO LINE (see earlier listing), except:
- One angled black four-polepiece pickup and one black eight-polepiece large pickup.
- Three controls (volume, balance, tone); passive circuit (active option from 2008).
- Black-plated hardware.

Also five-string version (2007–current).

STREAMER

STREAMER *See later STREAMER STAGE I listing.*

STREAMER BOLT-ON 1993–96 *Bolt-on neck, concave back/convex front body, one split and one straight pickup, four controls.*
Similar to STREAMER STAGE I (see later listing), except:
- Bolt-on neck.
- Four controls (volume, balance, two tone).
- Chrome-plated hardware.

Also five-string version (1993–96).
Also six-string version (1994–96).

STREAMER CORVETTE LTD 1991 *Body with f-holes.*
Similar to STREAMER STAGE I (see later listing), except:
- Semi-solid body with two f-holes; natural only.
- One black plain pickup and two black plain adjoining pickups.
- Four controls (volume, balance, two tone)
- Gold-plated hardware.

Limited edition of 125.

STREAMER CT 2004–07 *Model name on headstock.*
Similar to STREAMER LX (see later listing), except:
- Ebony fingerboard; chrome finish-face headstock.
- Body various chrome finish colours.

Also five-string version (2004–07).
Also six-string version (2004–07).
Custom Shop from 2008

STREAMER DOUBLE-BUCK ($$) 2006–current *Streamer $$ on headstock.*
Similar to STREAMER LX (see later listing), except:
- Two black eight-polepiece pickups.
- Four controls (volume, balance, two tone) and two mini-switches; active circuit.
- Gold- or black-plated hardware.

Also five-string version (2006–current).

STREAMER LX 1995–current *Model name on headstock.*
Similar to STREAMER BOLT-ON (see earlier listing), except:
- Chrome- or gold-plated hardware.
Also five-string version (1995–current).
Also six-string version (1995–current).
Also 30-inch short-scale version (2001–03).
Also 32-inch medium-scale version (2001–03).
Also 35-inch extra long-scale version (2001–03).

STREAMER LX JAZZMAN 2000–current *Model name on headstock.*
Similar to STREAMER LX (see earlier listing), except:
- One angled black eight-polepiece pickup and one black eight-polepiece large pickup.
- One dual-concentric control (volume/balance), three controls (all tone) and mini-switch.
- Gold-plated hardware.
Also five-string version (2000–current).

STREAMER LX LIMITED 2008 Two wood-cover pickups.
Similar to STREAMER LX (see earlier listing), except:
- Ebony fingerboard; eagle head inlay at 12th fret.
- Natural only.
- Two wood-cover pickups.
- Two dual concentric controls (volume/balance, treble/bass), one control (middle), three-way selector and two mini-switches.
- Black-plated hardware.
Also five-string version (2008).

STREAMER LX SHORT SCALE *See earlier STREAMER LX listing.*

STREAMER LX MEDIUM SCALE *See earlier STREAMER LX listing.*

STREAMER LX XTRA LONG SCALE *See earlier STREAMER LX listing.*

STREAMER PRO M 1995–2001 *Model name on headstock.*
Similar to STREAMER LX (see earlier listing), except:
- Two black plain adjoining pickups.
- Three dual-concentric controls (volume/balance, two treble/bass); later two controls (volume, balance) and one dual-concentric control (treble/bass).

- Gold-plated hardware.
Also five-string version (1995–2001).

STREAMER STAGE I 1985–current *Through-neck, concave-back/convex-front body, one split and one straight pickup, four controls.*
- Through-neck with wenge fingerboard (ebony option; fretless ebony option), dot markers (no markers from 1991).
- Double-cutaway concave-back/convex-front body; sunburst, natural or colours.
- One black split pickup and one black straight pickup.
- Four controls (volume, balance, two tone); later three controls (volume, balance, midrange) and one dual-concentric control (treble/bass); one dual-concentric control (volume/balance) and three controls (all tone) (1993–current); active circuit.
- Four-saddle bridge/tailpiece (four-saddle bridge, tailpiece from 1986).
- Gold- or black-plated hardware.
Known as STREAMER (1984–85).
Known as STREAMER STAGE I CLASSIC LINE (1993–94).
Also five-string version (1986–current).
Also six-string version (1987–current).
Also special-order seven-, eight-, ten- and twelve-string versions (Custom Shop from 2001).

STREAMER STAGE I 1989 LIMITED EDITION
1989 *One black plain pickup, two dual-concentric controls.*
Similar to STREAMER STAGE 1 (see earlier listing), except:
- Natural only.
- One black plain pickup.
- Two dual-concentric controls (volume/balance, treble/bass).
- Gold-plated hardware.
Limited edition of 120.

STREAMER STAGE I 1990 LIMITED EDITION 1990
Two black plain pickups.
Similar to STREAMER STAGE 1 (see earlier listing), except:
- Ebony fingerboard, no markers.
- Natural only.
- Two black plain pickups.
- Four controls (volume, balance, two tone).
- Gold-plated hardware.
Limited edition of 120.

STREAMER STAGE I CLASSIC LINE *See earlier*
STREAMER STAGE I listing.

STREAMER STAGE II 1986–current *Ornate large dot*
markers, two straight pickups.
Similar to STREAMER STAGE I (see earlier listing), except:
- Ornate large dot markers.
- Two black straight pickups.
- Gold-plated hardware.
Also five-string version (1987–current).
Also special-order six-, seven-, eight-, ten- and twelve-
string versions (Custom Shop fro 2001).

STREAMER STAGE II JACKI REZNICEK
SIGNATURE five-string 2006 *Five strings, signature on*
headstock.
Similar to STREAMER STAGE II (see earlier listing),
except:
- Ebony fingerboard, no markers; 34in scale, 26 frets;
  three-plus-two tuners with metal keys; Jacki Reznicek
  signature on headstock.
- Black only.
- One black plain split pickup and one black plain
  straight pickup.
- Two controls (volume, balance), one dual-concentric
  control (treble/bass) and two mini-switches.
- Five-saddle bridge, tailpiece.
- Black-plated hardware.
Custom Shop from 2007.

STREAMER STAGE II JIMMY EARL SIGNATURE
five-string 1993 *Five-strings, signature on headstock.*
Similar to STREAMER STAGE II (see earlier listing),
except:
- Maple fingerboard, no markers; three-plus-two tuners
  with metal keys; Jimmy Earl signature on headstock.
- Black or white.
- One dual-concentric control (volume/balance) and
  three controls (all tone).
- Five-saddle bridge, tailpiece.
- Gold-plated hardware.

STREAMER STAGE II P-NUT SIGNATURE five-string
2005 *Five strings, signature on headstock, chrome-plated*
hardware.
Similar to STREAMER STAGE II (see earlier listing),
except:
- Spiral markers; three-plus-two tuners with metal keys;
  P-Nut signature on headstock.

- One angled black eight-polepiece pickup and one
  black eight-polepiece large pickup.
- One dual-concentric control (volume/balance), three
  controls (all tone) and mini-switch.
- Five-saddle bridge, tailpiece.
- Chrome-plated hardware.
Limited edition of 46.
Custom Shop from 2006.

STREAMER STAGE II P-NUT II SIGNATURE five-
string 2007 *Five-strings, signature on headstock, black-*
plated hardware.
Similar to STREAMER STAGE II P-NUT SIGNATURE (see
earlier listing), except:
- Drop tuner on B string.
- Black-plated hardware.
Limited edition of 56.
Custom Shop from 2008.

STREAMER STANDARD ONE-PICKUP 1999–2002
Streamer Std on headstock, one pickup.
- Bolt-on neck with wenge fingerboard, no position
  markers.
- Contoured double-cutaway body; natural or colours.
- One black plain pickup.
- Two controls (volume, tone); front-mounted jack
  socket.
- Four-saddle bridge/tailpiece.
- Chrome-plated hardware.
Also five-string version (1999–2002).

STREAMER STANDARD TWO-PICKUP 1999–2002
Streamer Std on headstock, two pickups.
Similar to STREAMER STANDARD ONE-PICKUP (see
earlier listing), except:
- Two black plain pickups.
- Three controls (two volume, one tone).
Also five-string version (1999–2002).

STREAMER 5th ANNIVERSARY LTD 1987 *Block*
marker at 24th fret; two split pickups.
Similar to STREAMER STAGE I (see later listing), except:
- Ebony fingerboard; serial number in block marker at
  24th fret.
- Two black split pickups (one reversed).
- Two controls (volume, balance) and one dual-
  concentric control (treble/bass).
- Gold-plated hardware.
Limited edition of 30.

THUMB

THUMB 1985–current *Model name on headstock.*

- Through-neck with wenge (later ebony) fingerboard; fretless ebony option), dot markers (no markers from 1991); 34in scale, 26 frets.
- Double-cutaway concave-back/convex-front body; natural or colours.
- Two black pickups (one angled at bridge).
- Two controls (volume, balance) and one dual-concentric control (treble/bass); later two dual-concentric controls (volume/balance, treble/bass) and one control (middle); active circuit.
- Four-saddle bridge/tailpiece (four-saddle bridge, tailpiece from 1986).
- Black-, chrome- or gold-plated hardware.

Also five-string version (1986–current).
Also six-string version (1987–current).
Also special-order seven-, eight-, ten- and twelve-string versions (Custom Shop from 2001).

THUMB BOLT-ON (BO) 1993–current *Model name on headstock.*
Similar to THUMB (see earlier listing), except:
- Bolt-on neck with wenge fingerboard (fretless ebony option); 24 frets.
- Two controls (volume, balance) and one dual-concentric control (treble/bass).
- Black- or chrome-plated hardware.

Also five-string version (1993–current).
Also six-string version (1994–current).

THUMB BOLT-ON LIMITED EDITION 2001 *Bolt-on neck, ebony fingerboard.*
Similar to THUMB BOLT-ON (see earlier listing), except:
- Ebony fingerboard.
- Black-plated hardware.

Limited edition of 150.

THUMB BOLT-ON BLEACHED BLOND LIMITED EDITION 2003 *Maple fingerboard, mountain/moon markers.*
Similar to THUMB BOLT-ON (see earlier listing), except:
- Maple fingerboard, mountain/moon markers.
- Natural only.
- Chrome- or black-plated hardware.

Limited edition of 350.
Custom Shop from 2004

THUMB BOLT-ON DIRTY BLOND LIMITED EDITION 2006 *Bird markers.*

Similar to THUMB BOLT-ON (see earlier listing), except:
- Ebony fingerboard, bird markers.
- Natural only.
- One black plain split pickup and two black plain adjoining pickups.
- Two dual-concentric controls (volume/balance, treble/bass) and one control (middle).
- Black-plated hardware.

Also five-string version (2006).
Limited edition of 250.
Custom Shop from 2007.

THUMB BOLT-ON FLAMIN' BLOND LTD 2007 LIMITED EDITION 2007 *Model name on headstock*
Similar to THUMB BOLT-ON (see earlier listing), except:
- Ebony fingerboard, red flame markers.
- Natural only.
- One slim black eight-polepiece pickup (angled) and one large black eight-polepiece pickup.
- One dual-concentric control (volume/balance), three controls (all tone) and mini-switch.
- Black-plated hardware.

Limited edition of 300.
Custom Shop from 2008.

THUMB JACK BRUCE SIGNATURE first version
1988 *'Jack Bruce' on fingerboard.*
Similar to THUMB (see earlier listing), except:
- Ebony fingerboard (fretless option); 'Jack Bruce' and number in block inlay on fingerboard.
- Two black plain pickups.
- Two controls (volume, balance), one dual-concentric control (treble/bass) and mini-switch.
- Black-plated hardware.

Limited edition of 50.

THUMB JACK BRUCE SIGNATURE second version
1992 *Signature on body, one dual-concentric control.*
Similar to THUMB (see earlier listing), except:
- Ebony fingerboard (fretless option).
- Jack Bruce signature on body.
- Two black plain pickups.
- Two controls (volume, balance), one dual-concentric control (treble/bass) and mini-switch.
- Black-plated hardware.

Limited edition of 100 (50 fretted, 50 fretless).

THUMB JACK BRUCE SIGNATURE third version
2002–current *Body signature, 2 dual-concentric controls.*

Similar to THUMB (see earlier listing), except:

- Ebony fingerboard (fretless option).
- Jack Bruce signature on body.
- Two black plain pickups.
- Two dual-concentric controls (volume/balance, treble/bass), one control (middle) and mini-switch.
- Black-plated hardware.

Limited edition of 100 (50 fretted, 50 fretless).

Also CUSTOM SHOP versions from 2000
Also ROCK BASS versions of CORVETTE and STREAMER from 2002

Other basses produced by Warwick include:
Buzzard series 1984-current
Dolphin series 1989-current
FNA series 1998-current
Fortress series 1991-2000
Infinity series 2000-current
Katana series 2004-current
Nobby Meidel headless 1983-89
Nobby Meidel headless reissue 2008-current
Stryker 2004-current
Vampyre series 2003-current

YAMAHA

Japan / Taiwan

BB-5000 1984–88 *Five-string, through-neck, oval markers, solid contoured double-cutaway body, one split and one straight pickup in metal surrounds.*

- Through-neck with ebony fingerboard, oval markers; 34–inch scale, 24 frets; truss-rod adjuster at body end; four-and-one tuners with metal keys.
- Solid contoured double-cutaway body; colours.
- One split pickup and one straight pickup.
- Two controls (volume, tone) and three-way selector, all on body; side-mounted jack socket.
- Five-saddle bridge/tailpiece.
- Gold-plated hardware.

Other basses produced by Yamaha include:
Attitude series 1990–current
BB series 1978–current
MB series 1986–
RBX series 1986–current
TRB series 1989–current

Index

Entries with page numbers between 136 and 172 refer to the Reference Section. Page numbers in *italics* refer to illustrations.

Acknowledgements

INSTRUMENT OWNERS

Basses photographed came from the collections of the following individuals and organisations, and we are grateful for their help. The owners are listed here in the alphabetical order of the code used to identify their instruments in the Key that follows.

AA Adrian Ashton; **AG** Arbiter Group; **AJ** Anthony Jackson; **AM** Albert Molinaro; **AR** Alan Rogan; **BB** Boz Burrell estate; **BC** The Bass Centre, London; **BD** Bob Daisley; **CC** Chinery Collection; **DE** Duane Eddy; **DM** Dave Merlane; **DQ** Danny Quatrochi; **FE** Fender Great Britain & Ireland; **FF** Fausto Fabi; **GE** Giddy-Up-Einstein; **GG** Geoff Gould; **GP** Guy Pratt; **HK** Hap Kuffner; **HR** Hard Rock Cafe, London; **JB** Jack Bruce; **JE** John Entwistle; **JR** Jim Roberts; **JS** James Sims; **MA** Michael Anthony; **MF** Mo Foster; **MG** Music Ground; **MM** Marcus Miller; **MP** Maurice Preece; **PD** Paul Day; **PG** Peavey Guitars; **PH** Phil Harris; **PM** Paul McCartney; **PW** Paul Westwood; **RF** Rock Factory; **RG** Robin Guthrie; **RH** Randy Hope-Taylor; **SB** Sam Benjamin; **SC** Stanley Clarke; **SP** Steve Partlett; **TB** Tony Bacon; **WG** Warwick Gmbh.

KEY TO INSTRUMENT PHOTOGRAPHS

The following key is designed to identify who owned which basses at the time they were photographed. After the relevant bold-type page number(s) we've listed the brand or model followed by the owner's initials (see Instrument Owners above). For example, '24 Danelectro, DE' means that the Danelectro shown on page 24 was owned by Duane Eddy.

18–19 Precision, JE. **22–23** Gibson Electric Bass, JE; EB-2, AR. **26** Danelectro, DE. **26–27** Bass VI, JE. **27** Danelectro, AR. **30–31** 4001S, PD; 4000, MA. **34–35** '57 Precision, BD; '54 Precision, BC. **38–39** '60 Jazz, AR. **39** Harmony, MP; Jazz, JE. **42** '64 Jazz, GP. **42–43** '66 Precision, JE. **43** '63 Precision, BD; '66 Jazz, AA. **46–47** '56 Hofner, BC; '63 Hofner, PM. **50** Precision, FE. **50–51** Rick, PM. **54** Tele, RG. **54–55** Bass V, DM; Mustang, BC. **58–59** EB-3, PH; T'bird, JE. **62–63** AEB-1, FF. **63** ASB-1, JE. **66–67** Ampeg, CC; Hagstrom, BC; Gibson, RF. **70–71** Spider, JE. **71** No.1, GE; 8-string, HR. **74–75** Spector, AM. **75** Alembic, SC; Kramer, MF. **82** Steinberger, HK; Status, BC. **82–83** Steinberger, BC. **86–87** Fodera, AJ; Kubicki, BC.

90 Ken Smith, BC. **90–91** Modulus, GG. **94–95** StingRay, SP. **95** StingRay 5, BC. **98–99** Precision, JS. **99** Tele, TB; Jazz, MG. **102–103** Jazz, FE; Precision, BC. **106** Ibanez, DQ. **106–107** Yamaha, MG. **107** Aria, BC. **110–111** Jazz, RH. **111** Precision, FE. **114–115** Jazz, MM. **118** Martin, JR; Ashbory, PW. **118–119** Precision, BC. **122** Jazz, SB. **122–123** Roland, MA. **123** Urge, AG. **126** Peavey, PG; Thumb, JB. **126–127** Corvette, WG. **127** Lakland, BB. **130–131** Precision, FE. **131** Variax, BC.

Principal guitar photography is by Miki Slingsby, with some additional shots by Garth Blore and Nigel Bradley.

ARTIST PICTURES are identified by bold-type page number, subject, and photographer/agency. **27** Bruce, Jan Persson/Redfern's. **31** Jones, GAB Archives/Redfern's. **38** Osborn, richardandkarencarpenter.com. **46** McCartney & Lennon, Tony Gale/Pictorial Press. **50** Chandler, Pictorial Press; McCartney, Pictorial Press. **51** Jamerson, Rex Features. **59** Entwistle, Chris Morphet/Redfern's; Jones, Jorgen Angel/Redfern's. **67** Wyman, Richard Upper/Redfern's. **74** Clarke, Richard E. Aaron/Redfern's. **83** Lee, Pictorial Press. **87** Jackson, Andrew Lepley/Redfern's. **90** Squire, Fin Costello/Redfern's. **91** Bootsy, Fin Costello /Redfern's; Glover, Fotex/Redfern's; Barrett, Ian Dickson/Redfern's. **95** Johnson, Keith Bernstein/Redfern's. **103** Pastorius, Clayton Call/Redfern's. **106** Sting, Peter Noble/Redfern's. **107** East, Maryanne Bilham/Redfern's; Taylor, Pictorial Press. **114** Miller, David Redfern/Redfern's. **115** Burton, Pete Cronin/Redfern's; King, David Redfern/Redfern's. **119** Sandman, Ebet Roberts/Redfern's. **122** Moroder, GAB Archives/Redfern's. **127** LoMenzo, Gary Wolstenholme/Redfern's. **130** Wooten, Andrew Lepley/Redfern's. **131** Flea, Stefan M. Prager/Redfern's.

MEMORABILIA illustrated in this book, including advertisements, brochures, catalogues, colour charts, patents, and photographs (in fact anything that isn't a bass), comes from the Balafon Image Bank.

ORIGINAL INTERVIEWS

We are very grateful to the many people who agreed to be interviewed especially for The Bass Book. Interviews with the following were conducted by

THE BASS BOOK

Tony Bacon (for this and/or the first edition): Dave Bronze (Apr 94); Rick Danko (Jan 95); Danny Ferrington (Jan 95); George Fullerton (Feb 92); Dale Hyatt (Nov 94); Bobby Jones (Nov 07); Ted McCarty (Oct 92); Jaco Pastorius (Jul 76); Jay Piccirillo (Nov 07); Don Randall (Nov 94); Forrest White (Feb 92); Hans-Peter Wilfer (Nov 07). Interviews with the following were conducted by Tony Bacon & Barry Moorhouse in Nov and Dec 94 for the first (and subsequently this) edition: Nathan Daniel; Vinnie Fodera; Geoff Gould; Anthony Jackson; Jimmy Johnson; Dennis Kager; Paul McCartney; Jess Oliver; Ken Smith; Stuart Spector; Ned Steinberger; Carl Thompson; Rick Turner; Ron Wickersham. The sources of any previously published quotations are footnoted where they occur in the text.

THANKS to the following for help on this and the previous edition: American Federation of Musicians (Los Angeles, Nashville, New York); Tony Arambarri (NAMM); Dennis Anthony; Bob Archigian (LaBella); Andy Babiuk; Paul Bechtoldt; Bob Bernstein (Hard Rock); John Blaney; Andrew Bodnar; Bruce Bolen; Julie Bowie; Russell Bowner (Hard Rock London); Craig Brody; Boz Burrell; Dave Burrluck (Guitarist); Calloway Editions; Mike Carey; Walter Carter (Gruhn Guitars); Trevor Cash; Craig DeFalco; André Duchossoir; Latrice Epps; Jason Farrell (Fender Musical Instruments); Howard Fields; Vinnie Fodera; Roger Forrester; Bert Gerecht; Dave Good (House Music); Martin Gravestock (Bass Centre London); Alan Greenwood; Dave Gregory; John Hammel; Clay Harrell; Rick Harrison (Music Ground); Richard Henry; Christopher Hjort; Steve Hodgkinson; Mikael Jansson; Stan Jay (Mandolin Bros); the Jeep (not a van); Scott Jennings (Route 66 Guitars); Chris Jisi; Bill Kaman; Dixie Kidd; Dan Lakin; Scott Malandrone; Russ McFee (GHS); John McLaren Jr. (G&L); Gareth Morgan; Tony Moscal (St Louis Music); Gill Moorhouse; Hans Moust; Christiane Neerhut (Bert Kaempfert Music); Russell North (Fender UK & Ireland); Jim Otell; Nick Owen (Bass Centre London); Jason Padgitt (Fender Musical Instruments); Vincent Pelote (Institute of Jazz Studies, Rutgers); Bob Pridden; Ian Purser; Heinz Rebellius; Julian Ridgway (Redfern's); Rob Rizzuto (G&L); Alan Rogan; Howard Satterley; Martin Scott; Keith Smith; Pete 'The Fish' Stevens (Wal); Ray Todd (Strings & Things); Rob Turner (EMG); Bud Tutmarc; Ariana Urbout (MTV); Chris Ward (Bass Centre London); Neil Whitcher (Fender UK & Ireland); Mica Wickersham (Alembic).

SPECIAL THANKS to Paul Day for the splendidly updated and reorganised reference section.

BOOKS

Adrian Ashton The Bass Handbook (Backbeat 2005) Good all-in-one guide to playing, hardware, and other stuff.

Andy Babiuk Beatles Gear revised edition (Backbeat 2002) Definitive work on their basses, guitars, keyboards, amps, etc.

Tony Bacon 50 Years Of Fender (Balafon/Miller Freeman 2000) Year by year through basses, guitars, and amps.

Tony Bacon The Fender Electric Guitar Book (Backbeat 2007) History of guitars only: Strats, Teles, and the rest.

Tony Bacon & Barry Moorhouse The Bass Book (Balafon/Miller Freeman 1995) First edition of the book you hold, but shorter story, different pic selection, different ref section.

Tony Bacon & Gareth Morgan Paul McCartney Bassmaster: Playing The Great Beatles Basslines (Backbeat 2006) Full story of Macca's prowess as fabs bassman, plus nine transcriptions.

Tony Bacon & Paul Day The Rickenbacker Book (Miller Freeman 1994) History of guitars only.

Tony Bacon & Paul Day The Ultimate Guitar Book (DK/Knopf 1991) General guitar history including basses.

Paul Bechtoldt G&L: Leo's Legacy (Woof 1994) Slim look at Leo's post-Fender post-Music Man company.

J.W. Black & Albert Molinaro The Fender Bass: An Illustrated History (Hal Leonard 2001) Good pictorial chronology including detail on feature changes.

Klaus Blasquiz The Fender Bass (Hal Leonard undated) Slim and rather muddled early attempt at the story.

Karl Coryat (editor) The Bass Player Book (Miller Freeman 1999) Collection of interviews plus playing/gear features from Bass Player mag.

André Duchossoir Gibson Electrics – The Classic Years (Hal Leonard 1994) Detailed history, including basses, to 1965.

Joe Dunn Hofner Violin 'Beatle' Bass (River 1996) Slim history.

George Fullerton Guitar Legends (Centerstream 1993) Story of author's time at Fender, G&L.

George Gruhn & Walter Carter Gruhn's Guide To Vintage Guitars (GPI 1991) Detailed IDs, chronologies for many collectable brands, including some basses.

Greg Hopkins & Bill Moore Ampeg: The Story Behind The Sound (Hal Leonard 1999) Detailed and info-packed account.

Chris Jisi (ed) Brave New Bass (Backbeat 2003) Thirty interviews from Bass Player mag.

Dr Licks Standing In The Shadows Of Motown (Dr Licks 1989) Admirable work on James Jamerson.

Bill Milkowski Jaco: The Extraordinary And Tragic Life Of Jaco Pastorius (Backbeat 2005) Good detailed biography.

Tom Mulhern (editor) Bass Heroes (GPI 1993) Thirty interviews from Bass Player mag.

Jim Roberts How The Fender Bass Changed The World (Backbeat 2001) Good history, especially on players.

Jim Roberts American Basses: An Illustrated History & Player's Guide (Backbeat 2003) Plenty of info in an A-to-Z of U.S. brands.

Richard R. Smith Fender: The Sound Heard 'Round The World (Garfish 1995) Well researched view of early history; good photos and some bass material.

Tom Wheeler American Guitars (HarperPerennial 1990) Wide-ranging U.S. guitar history including basses.

Forrest White Fender: The Inside Story (GPI 1994) Account of author's time at Fender, Music Man.

MAGAZINES

We consulted back issues of the following magazines: Bass (Japan); Bass Guitar Magazine (U.K.); Bass Player (U.S.); Beat Instrumental (U.K.); Beat Monthly (U.K.); Down Beat (U.S.); Guitar & Bass Magazine (U.K.); Guitar Player (U.S.); Guitarist (U.K.); Making Music (U.K.); Melody Maker (U.K.); Mojo (U.K.); Record Collector (U.K.); The Music Trades (U.S.); Rolling Stone (U.S.); Vintage Gallery (U.S.); Vintage Guitar Magazine (U.S.); 20th Century Guitar (U.S.).

TRADEMARKS

Throughout this book we have mentioned a number of registered trademark names. Rather than put a trademark or registered symbol next to every occurrence of a trademarked name, we state here that we are using the names only in an editorial fashion and that we do not intend to infringe any trademarks.

UPDATES?

The authors and publisher welcome any new information for future editions. Email us at bassbook@jawbonepress.com or write to The Bass Book, Backbeat U.K., 2A Union Court, 20–22 Union Road, London SW4 6JP, England.

"I think you lose a certain amount of your naive, original voice when you get too technical. It happens in every art form."

ERIC AVERY, JANE'S ADDICTION